Inspiration and Healing

Letters with LDS (Mormon) Missionaries

David S. Dewey

Copyright © 2014 by David S. Dewey
All rights reserved. No part of this book may be reproduced, scanned, photocopied or distributed in any printed or electronic form without written permission from the copyright holder. The views expressed herein are the responsibility of the author and do not necessarily represent the position of the Church of Jesus Christ of Latter-day Saints.
First Edition: December 2014
Printed in the United States of America
ISBN: 978-0-692-31295-7

Front cover photograph by David and Jessie ©Some Rights Reserved by treasuresthouhast (CC BY 2.0); https://flickr.com/photos/74568056/L; horizontal flip; Angel Moroni atop Mormon Temple Spire, Salt Lake City.
Cover background image designed by Alberto Ziveri ©Some Rights Reserved (CC BY 2.0); https://flickr.com/photos/6493621231/L; Wallpaper for ipad.
Back cover reference: Doctrine and Covenants 50:22

Dedications

This book is dedicated to the amazing cadre of valiant missionaries who selflessly serve as emissaries of the Lord Jesus Christ throughout the world and to their devoted families and friends who love and sustain them.

And to all who suffer, may you find God's healing and comfort through service to others in whatever form it may take.

Acknowledgements

Thank you to Gary, Bonnie and Lucile for their contributions to the title and cover design for this book.

I wish to acknowledge the kind persuasive skills of Irinna for convincing me that this story was inspirational and worthy of wider exposure.

I express gratitude for all of the family members and friends who supported me with letters during my full-time missionary service as a young man in northern England so many years ago.

I especially want to thank "my missionaries" for kindly enduring my unrelenting letters and for the beautiful letters they wrote to me in return. They have no idea how much joy I felt from them and how therapeutic they were.

Finally, neither my letter writing nor this book would have been possible were it not for the incredible care and encouragement provided to me by my devoted wife, Bonnie, during these past several years in particular; and for the support of my immediate and extended family members and many friends.

Table of Contents

Acknowledgements..iv
Preface..vii
Introduction..1
Letter One
   "It's All True!"... 17
Letter Two
   Inspiration from the Holy Ghost.. 23
Letter Three
   God is Looking Over You and His Work 29
Letter Four
   Living Prophets... 33
Letter Five
   Selfless Service 39
Letter Six
   Inspired Mission Presidents... 43
Letter Seven
   A Missionary's Sacrifice 47
Letter Eight
   The Restoration of the Gospel 51
Letter Nine
   You are Where You are For a Reason 55
Letter Ten
   Priesthood Authority 59

Letter Eleven
  Is Your Heart Right?..63
Letter Twelve
  State of Becoming..67
Letter Thirteen
  Have Fun...71
Letter Fourteen
  Pray Constantly...75
Letter Fifteen
  Working Toward Perfection...79
Letter Sixteen
  The Standard of Truth Will Prevail.......................................83
Letter Seventeen
  Working for the Living and the Dead...................................87
Letter Eighteen
  Modern Apostles and Prophets...91
Letter Nineteen
  Miracles Accompany This Work..95
Letter Twenty
  Sanctification...99
Letter Twenty-One
  Angels Assist with This Work..103
Letter Twenty-Two
  What is a Missionary?...107
Appendix A 115
Appendix B...117
Notes..119

Preface

Dear Reader,

Greetings and salutations! This book is about the power of inspiration and healing through the medium of letters. Letters of inspiration, written by a physically ailing man in great pain but with a strong testimony of the restored Gospel of Jesus Christ and a lifetime of experience, sent to young inexperienced Mormon missionaries who responded to calls from a modern prophet to "hasten the work" of building up the Kingdom of God on the earth. Return letters of healing, written by young men and women with rapidly growing and strengthening testimonies of Gospel truth gained through selfless service to strangers around the world who they had come to love, sent to a man in his pain and disability. Letters wherein each gave of himself or herself to the other. Letters filled with stories and experiences, doctrine and testimony, support and love.

The chapters of this book are a succession of monthly letters I faithfully wrote to the young missionaries who had been called to serve full-time LDS missions, primarily from my home ward congregation, which I began sending after they had completed their instruction at the Missionary Training Center and had arrived at their assigned field of labor. The letters were written during the years of my slow healing and recovery from a severe debilitating illness.

Prior to their missionary service (at ages ranging from eighteen to twenty-one), several of these young men, in their capacities in Aaronic Priesthood quorums, weekly brought the sacrament to me in our home when I was homebound due to my disability. In addition, my wife came to know and love many of these young men and women while she served as the teacher of their youth Sunday School class.

I remember from my own full-time missionary experience as a young man how important letters from home were, including letters from those who were other than family members who also cared. My primary focus in writing to these young people was to share some encouraging thoughts and perspectives on their service. This, when combined with stories from my own life and missionary experience, and emphasized with relevant quotes from others who have said things better than I can, supported the monthly topics and principles I addressed. If possible, I was desirous of inspiring and motivating "my missionaries" in some small way through my letters.

Following each letter printed here, I have included selected relevant excerpts from many of the letters the missionaries wrote back to me. Oh, how their letters touched my heart, distracted me from my suffering and contributed to my healing.

I have preserved the privacy of the missionaries by using brackets [ ] in lieu of their names and specific mission locations.

Please join us in peeking into our journey of inspiration and healing through letters.

Sincerely,

Brother Dewey

Introduction

Several years ago I was diagnosed with diabetes as a result of family genetics. One of the degenerative complications of many who suffer with this disease is neuropathy, or nerve pain, especially in the feet. Many diabetics experience little or no pain of this nature, as my mother and sister before me, but many others *do* suffer from this complication. I fell into the later group and accepted it as part of my lot in life.

However, within a few weeks of the diagnosis, the neuropathy grew more severe and was quickly spreading up from my feet into my legs. Before long, some of the symptoms had advanced into my upper body as well. As the pain increased and spread, my leg muscles weakened causing me to fall on several occasions. I was forced to use a walker around home for my own safety and my wife pushed me in a wheelchair when going out, which was primarily to doctor appointments. The pain and accompanying muscle weakness became debilitating.

For those who may be interested in the details of my diagnosis, the next four short paragraphs are the medical terms my neurologist used to describe my condition with their general definitions. You will see why I had such a difficult time explaining what I had when people inquired about it since I couldn't even pronounce half of these terms.

Distal sensory motor neuropathy (as seen in diabetes): A problem with the functioning of the nerves outside the spinal cord, which includes numbness, weakness and burning pain (especially at night).

Proximal diabetic amyotrophy: A radicul asymmetrical weakening and degeneration of muscles. A progressive wasting of muscle tissues combined with severe muscle pain.

Lumbosacral radiculoplexus neuropathy: A clinical condition characterized by debilitating pain, weakness and atrophy most commonly affecting the proximal thigh muscles asymmetrically. The syndrome is usually monophasic and proceeded by significant weight loss of at least 10 lbs. (I lost nearly 40 lbs.) With this condition recovery is gradual.

Diabetic Cachexia: A general physical wasting with loss of weight and muscle mass due to a disease, also known as marasmus; chronic weakness, debility (caused by illness).

I tell you about my illness only because it lays the groundwork that explains how I came to engage in my letter writing campaign to "my missionaries."

After a year or so of recovery, I had enough physical improvement that I could occasionally get out of the house using only a walker. On those Sundays when I was able to endure the pain long enough, I again began attending the sacrament meeting portion of the three-hour block of services at our LDS congregation with my wife. Perhaps six months later, I was asked by a member of the stake presidency to speak at the Saturday evening session of our upcoming stake conference. He requested that I speak about my health experience and what I had learned from it.

Initially I tried to decline the invitation because I was uncomfortable and embarrassed to deliver an entire talk about *me* and *my* problems when so many others have problems of their own which are equally significant to them. I was kindly informed there would be people in the congregation who needed to hear my story because it would be a help to them. On that basis I acquiesced and agreed to speak.

Preparing the message would be the easy part, since I was living it, but telling it in public would be an emotional experience to be sure. The more challenging part, however, would be physically standing for fifteen or twenty minutes to deliver the message. By that time I could walk for modest distances with the support of two walking poles, but the simple act of standing in place for that length of time, even holding on the pulpit for support, would be very painful and my legs would be weakened to the point that I could be at risk of falling.

With sheer willpower and, I believe, with divine help, I was able to stand long enough to deliver my sermon.

What follows is the text of that address with minor editing. I share it with you here to provide more details about my health challenge and what I have learned from it.

Introduction

Good evening my good brothers and sisters. I have always found much joy in sitting among a large gathering of Latter-day Saints, such as this, in stake conference. However, it's not quite as joyful from this perspective of standing in front of you. I'm humbled to have been invited to address you tonight. I want the members of the stake presidency to know that in spite of their foible in having me speak, they have my full faith and support and I love each of them.

They have asked me to address you somewhat concerning a challenge I've been experiencing recently and a sampling of what I have learned and gained from it. Please know that my story is incidental compared to others, whose burdens are much heavier than mine, and it is not meant to invoke sympathy. Rather, it's a celebration of our Heavenly Father's plan for our happiness and the great atoning sacrifice wrought in our behalf by our Savior, Jesus Christ.

My Illness

Almost two years ago, I started experiencing pain in my feet that we originally thought to be typical diabetic neuropathy. Within a couple of months, however, the pain significantly increased and progressed up my legs. Soon the pain had progressed into my torso, arms and hands, though not as severely. I was losing weight at a rapid rate. I was also losing so much strength in my legs that it was increasingly difficult for me to walk and I even fell several times. I was soon forced to use a walker at home and a wheelchair when going out.

My first neurologist, after having administered a battery of tests, couldn't determine the cause of my condition. She told my wife, when I wasn't in the room, that if the neuropathy and muscle weakness continued to spread to my lungs and heart, I could die.

My second neurologist was finally able to correctly diagnose that I had a rare neurological illness, which included all of its magnificent pain. He said he had good news and bad news. The bad news was that they didn't know the cause of the condition and there was nothing medical science could do for me; except to try to mitigate the pain. The good news was that my condition shouldn't get any worse and my body would begin to heal itself, for the most part, with some permanent nerve damage yet to be determined. I had gone from a prognosis of possible death to that of a significant recovery. My recovery, however, would take up to two years or more. Now, nineteen months later, you can see that I've improved.

During this difficult challenge, I often prayed that God would help me to endure it well and that I would be able to recognize the lessons that he wanted me to learn from the experience. I found that there were many things I needed to learn, not the least of which was patience.

Pain

Someone said that pain is God's megaphone to arouse a deaf world. If that's true, then I was getting a loud wake-up call. The pain took the forms of aching, stinging, burning, sensations of cold and hot, tingling, twitching, prickling, shooting electrical shocks, and, at its worst, the sensation of bugs crawling under the surface of my skin. Nerve pain is one of the most difficult pains to mask, so the regimen of pain medications I was prescribed merely took the edge off so I might better tolerate it. Unfortunately, the pain became worse at night making it very difficult to get any meaningful sleep. I don't mind telling you there were nights, when the pain was at its worst, that I prayed to God multiple times; pleading with Him to grant me, perhaps, an hour or two of sleep, to escape from the misery.

Prayer

I read a candidly personal observation about approaching God in prayer by Sister Wendy Ulrich that taught me something about my own prayers. She said, "I notice I am generally quite content to imagine God high in the heavens, listening from some far away throne room, in my very human prayers. If I try to imagine, instead, inviting God to come close, to enter my little room and be seated nearby, I can hardly tolerate the emotions inherent in the image. I stop him at the perimeter, and even then I am flooded with fears and tears. I feel an instinct to drop to my knees and protest with Isaiah [or Moses or the brother of Jared]. Yet, I want to move closer to God, even if doing so evokes potent feelings of unworthiness in all my most tender places. If I cannot now go where he is, will he yet come near to me?"[1]

Yes, He will and does come near to us. I am reminded of what Brother S. Michael Wilcox said, "The Savior is aware of our struggles, and He walks beside us many times, and waits for us to cry out, ['Where are you' or] 'Who are you?' To which He responds, 'I am [He] who has waited a long time for you to speak to me.'"[2]

Music

I have always been inspired by the hymns of the restoration of the gospel and the songs of Zion. President J. Reuben Clark Jr. said, "We get nearer to the Lord through music than perhaps through any other thing except prayer."[3]

And I have come to know how listening to inspired music is a helpful mask for pain. My favorite CD is now "Called to Serve" by the Mormon Tabernacle Choir and Orchestra at Temple Square. I honestly cannot tell you how many dozens and dozens of times I have listened to those inspiring hymns. They brought sweet tears of joy to my eyes, added strength to my testimony, and drew my mind away from my trials and the pain for a moment. I was especially touched and strengthened by the words in the 3rd and 7th verses of the Hymn "How Firm a Foundation" which spoke directly to my soul:

> Fear not, I am with thee; Oh *be not dismayed*,
> For I am thy God and will *still give thee aid*.
> *I'll strengthen thee, help thee, and cause thee to stand*,
> Upheld by my righteous, omnipotent hand.
>
> The soul that on Jesus hath leaned for repose
> I will not, I cannot, desert to his foes;
> That soul, though all hell should endeavor to shake,
> I'll never, no never, *no never forsake!*[4]

Fairness

Each morning after my miraculous diagnoses, I would arise, sit on the edge of the bed and stop to ascertain if I felt any improvement. But there was none. This went on for weeks, which turned into months. I fought emotional despondency almost daily. There were some days when the darkness won out.

After a few months of this, two things happened at about the same time that significantly changed my outlook and my ability to deal with my situation. First, I decided to stop asking myself each morning if I felt any improvement since the "no" answer only resulted in despondency. I determined when I arose in the morning I would simply get about my day and if and when I experienced any improvement, no matter how small, we would celebrate it, be grateful for it, and continue on with life.

Second, I read a biographical sketch in the *Church News* about a new member of the Second Quorum of the Seventy, Elder Larry W. Wilson.[5] The article described how he had suffered from an illness that appeared to be remarkably similar to what I was suffering from – and he recovered! Finally, here was someone I could relate to, who gave me great hope. I couldn't help writing him a letter to thank him for sharing his story because it helped me so much (see Appendix A).

During difficult and challenging times, we must resist the temptation to give up, to blame God, or to complain: "This isn't fair," or to ask "Why me?"

Brother Robert L. Millet explained, "Life isn't all about fairness. The idea of fairness is not a bad one... [but] sometimes the notion of fairness gets in our way prevent[ing] us from grasping much more profound and eternally relevant concepts... such supernal principles as mercy and grace.

"The Father's plan of salvation, the gospel of Jesus Christ, is not, strictly speaking, a plan of fairness. It is a system of mercy, an extension of grace. Baptist Pastor Charles Stanley taught: '[God] had to do something very unfair. He had to send his son to this earth to die for sins he didn't commit. Fairness would demand that we die for our own sins. But the good news is that God opted for grace and mercy over fairness.'"[6]

Tender Mercies and Angels

As a result of my inability to work and our depleting savings, my resilient wife, Bonnie, who had so dutifully cared for me and lovingly worried about me, had to go to work to help support us; this after more than three decades of being a full-time mother, homemaker, and more recently, a doting grandmother. We were able to find her employment through LDS Employment Services with the help of a ward member who was serving a Church Service Mission there at the time.

Our extended family members were so very supportive, kind, caring, and generous to us in many ways. There is nothing more important than a family who rallies around one another during times of need, and we love them for it.

Although we live modestly, we were still struggling financially. Finally, I did something I have never had to do before. I swallowed my male pride, hesitatingly picked up the phone, and in supplication called my loving High Priest Group Leader. He immediately "rallied the troops" who came to our aid. Our bishop and relief society president were particularly kind, understanding and helpful to us.

Again quoting Sister Ulrich, "Some of us aren't too keen about the idea of admitting our needs... The world esteems the powerful.

"[But] God does not deride human neediness as we do. Instead, he chastens us for our illusions of self-sufficiency."[7]

I received cards of encouragement, visits from Church leaders and members and from other friends. I was especially touched when a loaf of fresh baked bread was delivered to our home made by a sister in the ward who was struggling with her own serious life challenges. Another caring member of our ward exchanged books with me which were delivered by her husband whom we affectionately dubbed the "bookmobile." Our neighbors all expressed their concern and willingness to help in any way they could, including a kind neighbor lady who lit a candle for us in her Catholic Church. Several good friends from around the country have kept up with me and encouraged me by email.

We received priesthood blessings, our names were put on the prayer rolls of several temples, and many people prayed for us. I believe in all of these things and am confident they have all contributed to my recovery.

I can tell you that the spirit of service is alive and well in our family, ward and stake. We were served by so many in ways too numerous to mention here. Our Heavenly Father has extended to us many "tender mercies" either directly from heaven above or through earthly angels. You angels know who you are, and Bonnie and I love and appreciate you so much.

Missionary Letters

With the onset of my illness, I needed to be released from my Church callings since I was not able to perform them. I couldn't remember a time when I did not have a calling in the Church. After a short while I thought "surely there is something I can do." After all, the Lord in modern revelation has said, "Verily I say, men should be anxiously engaged in a good cause, and do many things of their own free will, and bring to pass much righteousness;" (D&C

58: 27). He also said, "Unto whom much is given much is required." (D&C 82:3).

While lying in bed I came up with the idea of writing letters to the full-time missionaries serving from our ward. As I remember from my own experience, missionaries love receiving letters from the home front. Perhaps I might serve them each month by providing a little encouragement and inspiration. As is usually the case when we provide service to others, my letter writing campaign took my mind off of my own problems for a while by giving me something positive to think about and work on all month long.

Brothers and sisters, I can scarcely tell you what a tremendously wonderful experience this has been for me. Although I made it clear in my letters to the missionaries that I didn't expect them to write back to me given their busy schedules, most did anyway. They said how good it was to know that someone from home, besides their families, remembered and cared for them. Some sent photos that adorn a wall in our computer room. Several even said there were times when what I had written must have been inspired because it was *just what they had needed, just when they needed it*. I am convinced, however, they did more for me, than I ever did for them.

Discipleship

Over the many months of my struggle, I also prayed that God would help me learn to become a better disciple of His Son, Jesus Christ, and to give me the strength to overcome my weaknesses in order to become such. I have read, studied, and learned much about discipleship, and have been trying to incorporate those principles into my life. May I share a few of these things with you?

Discipleship is not just a single epiphany moment, it is an ongoing exercise. What's more, it is an elevated life style developed moment by moment, day by day, even person by person. It's based on a true understanding of God's plan for us, and what we must do and what we must become to obtain His promised blessings.

King Benjamin, in the Book of Mormon, taught us to put off the natural man and become as a child, submissive, meek, humble, patient, full of love, and willing to submit to all things which the Lord sees fit to inflict upon us, even as a child submits to his father (Mosiah 3:19). Notice that submissiveness is mentioned twice.

And what about that word "inflict?" I have often pondered over just what it means in that context. Then I found that Elder Neal A. Maxwell had also pondered on it. He said: "I've thought often, as you doubtless have, of the significance of King Benjamin's use of the word 'inflict.' Not random challenges but customized challenges come to us, tutorial challenges, and the word 'inflict' assures, then, a tutorial and loving God… one whose purposes we will not always understand."

"Nephi said, in effect, I don't always know the meaning of all things, but I know God loves his children (1 Nephi 11:16-17). If you and I can know that, then we can bear up as sons and daughters of God when, in a customized way, things are inflicted upon us."

Elder Maxwell further taught, "In this process of discipleship, we soon learn it is an incremental process. There has to be attention to the seemingly ordinary things as well as the seemingly ordinary people. I conclude that there are no ordinary people [and] there are likewise no ordinary moments. …this is part of coming to comprehend what discipleship is all about. Sobering, therefore, is the only word I can use regarding the dimensions of daily discipleship."

He also pointed out that, "Jesus said 'Come unto me.' [And] promised, 'I will show you your weaknesses.' Reassuringly, however, some of those weaknesses, as the scriptures say, actually become strengths. And therein lays the essence of the process of discipleship. It is a process full of mercy and love, emblematic of Heavenly Father's plan of happiness. It is the effort of a loving Father God and his redeeming son, Jesus Christ, to do all they can do to help us during the crowded time provided in this short mortal classroom. To become like them involves both obedience to their ordinances and emulation of their attributes. All in order that we might return to them. No wonder, therefore, we are repeatedly urged to use our time wisely by forsaking the world and taking up the cross daily. It's a process that's unrelenting as far as I see."⁸

Sobering and unrelenting; these are the words chosen by an exemplary modern Apostle of the Lord Jesus Christ to describe the discipline of discipleship, as one who knows. The ancient prophet Moroni learned this from his life experience: "For ye receive not a witness until after the trial of your faith" (Ether 12:6).

"All In"- The Full Treatment

During these many months of endurance, I have come to appreciate, as never before, that true discipleship requires that we be *all in*. We can't merely be dangling a toe in, nor can we have one foot in Zion and the other in Babylon.

C.S. Lewis, the great English Christian apologist, wisely wrote, "When one gets involved with God, this loving tutor doesn't stop halfway through."And then he explained more fully what he meant by citing a humorous yet insightful story from his youth:

"When I was a child I often had a toothache, and I knew that if I went to my mother she would give me something which would deaden the pain for that night and let me get to sleep. But I did not go to my mother – at least, not till the pain became very bad. And the reason I did not go was this. I did not doubt she would give me the aspirin; but I knew she would also do something else. I knew she would take me to the dentist [the] next morning. I could not get what I wanted out of her without getting something more, which I did not want. I wanted immediate relief from pain: but I could not get it without having my teeth set permanently right. And I knew those dentists: I knew they started fiddling about with all sorts of other teeth which had not yet begun to ache. They would not let sleeping dogs lie, if you gave them an inch they took a [mile]."

Lewis continued, "Now, if I may put it in that way, Our Lord is like the dentist. If you give Him an inch, He will take a [mile]. ... people go to Him to be cured of some one particular sin which they are ashamed of, or which is obviously spoiling daily life. Well, He will cure it all right; but He will not stop there. That may be all you asked, but if once you call Him in, He will give you the full treatment."9

To be a true disciple of Christ, we must be ready and willing to humbly and courageously receive the "full treatment" because we know this is the only way in which God can mold us into the kind of beings we must become to be worthy to return to Him in the celestial kingdom after this earthly life of testing. We must have total trust in Him, confidence in Him, exercise a ready reliance upon Him, and serve Him faithfully. We have to be totally committed, or in other words, *all in*.

We learn in the Book of Moses 1:39 that God's "work and glory is to bring to pass the immortality and eternal life of man," and suffering, in part, serves that end. Lewis, without the benefit of modern scripture, astutely observed, "It seems to us all unnecessary, but that is because we have not yet had the slightest notion of the tremendous thing He means to make of us.

"We are bidden to put on Christ to become like God, [and] God intends to give us what we need, not what we now think we want."

Lewis continued, "The command to be ye perfect is not idealist... Nor is it a command to do the impossible. He is going to make us into creatures that can obey that command. He said (in the Bible) that we [can be] 'gods' and He is going to make good His words. If we let Him – for we can prevent Him, if we choose – He will make... us into a god or goddess... The process will be long, and in part very painful, but that is what we are in for. Nothing less. He meant what He said."[10]

What is that old phrase we sometimes hear? "No one said it would be easy, but that it would be worth it."

I conclude with one more beautiful thought expressed by Elder Maxwell, "If we are fully [faithful], the scriptures promise us that eventually we can know that sublime moment when we will be..., 'clasped in the arms of Jesus' at the entrance of his kingdom. If we truly yearn for that marvelous moment, then our discipleship will be persistent in daily life."[11]

My Testimony

My brothers and sisters, I testify to you that God, our Heavenly Father, lives and loves us. He wants us to call upon Him and He will provide us with exactly what we need.

His Only Begotten Son, Jesus Christ, came to earth at the meridian of time and wrought grace and mercy for us by His great and unimaginable atoning sacrifice.

I declare that Joseph Smith Jr., who ushered in the restoration of the Gospel, was, and is, a true Prophet of God in this dispensation of time. He translated the ancient plates by the gift and power of God producing the Book of Mormon. This great book is, indeed, another testament of Jesus Christ. And I testify that it is true.

I know that the Church of Jesus Christ of Latter-day Saints is the only true and living church on the face of the whole earth. It is alive in Christ and it breathes modern revelation by the Holy Ghost.

The truthfulness of these things has been made known to me by personal revelation from the Holy Ghost. This knowledge moves me to keep the commandments of God and to serve Him and my fellow beings. This knowledge enables me to more faithfully endure the vicissitudes of this mortal life until one day, I too, along with my dear eternal companion, hope to be cradled in the merciful arms of a loving God at the entrance to His high kingdom.

Of these things I declare and testify in the worthy name of our Lord and Savior, even Jesus Christ, amen.

At the conclusion of the meeting, I decided to "linger longer" on the stand to wait for most of the congregation to leave the chapel before I tried to carefully navigate my way out of the building on weakened legs. Soon a few folks made their way onto the stand to shake my hand and thank me for my talk. Some of them I knew and others I did not know. I then noticed a line of people had formed to greet me. So many of them commented about how inspirational my words had been for them. This spontaneous outpouring of love caught me by surprise and brought tears of gratitude and joy to my eyes. It was a good while before I was able to make my way out of the stake center that evening.

About three months after I had spoken in stake conference, I had a most unexpected surprise. I was contacted by Irinna Danielson, Senior Executive Producer for *Mormon Times TV,* a local television program which aired on Sunday mornings after the Mormon Tabernacle Choir broadcast on KSL-TV Channel 5. They had heard about how I was writing to the missionaries during my disability and wanted to do a feature about it on their program. She believed it to be inspiring. Although I was admittedly flattered, I tried to discourage her because I considered my effort to be a modest activity that was insignificant compared to the kinds of stories they had reported on. But she was persistent.

I suggested that perhaps she might talk to two of three of *my* missionaries, who had recently returned from their honorable missions, about what impact, if any, my letters might have had on them during their missions. If they responded by saying that my letters had, in fact, added any real value to them then I will agree to an interview, but only if she would include them in the program in some way since I was reluctant to talk about myself. Honestly, I thought she would balk at having to go to that much trouble to get such an unpretentious story. To my dismay she responded by saying, "…that is a great idea to include some of 'your' missionaries. I will give them a call and then approach you again about possibly doing a story with you and them. We never think that the things that we do are very significant, but sometimes the small things can have a big impact on someone else. I'll let you think about it. I'll be in touch soon."[12]

When I didn't hear from her for over two weeks, I presumed the matter was over and done. Then I received another email message from her: "You're in luck! You're an inspiration. I have contacted your missionaries and they had nothing but great things to say about the impact that your letters had on their missions. I would still love to do a story about all of you – from the perspective of the letter writer and the letter receivers.

"Is there a date in the next month or so that would work with your schedule for us to come out to your home and interview you and your missionaries about the experience? They've agreed to bring the letters that you wrote them, and I think it would just be a beautiful representation of how through small and simple things, great things can come to pass."[13]

Well, a deal is a deal; I was now committed to do the interview. A time was arranged when the three returned missionaries and I could all get together at my home. Irinna came to our home and conducted the interviews with us while a cameraman filmed it all. They made it a painless experience.

A few days before the television program aired, the host of the program, Michelle King, in her weekly newspaper column in the *Deseret News*, wrote the following introduction to the episode: "Also on April 14th – the power of the written word and how it changed several lives. You'll see how a local man's debilitating illness motivated him to step it up and support young LDS missionaries serving from his congregation."[14]

Should you desire, you may view the Mormon Times TV piece online. It's entitled "The power of letters" and can be found at www.youtube.com/user/MormonTimes.

Now behold, a marvelous work is about to come forth among the children of men.

Therefore, O ye that embark in the service of God, see that ye serve him with all your heart, might, mind and strength, that ye may stand blameless before God at the last day.

Therefore, if ye have desires to serve God ye are called to the work;

For behold the field is white already to harvest; and lo, he that thrusteth in his sickle with his might, the same layeth up in store that he perisheth not, but bringeth salvation to his soul;

And faith, hope, charity and love, with an eye single to the glory of God, qualify him for the work.

Remember faith, virtue, knowledge, temperance, patience, brotherly kindness, godliness, charity, humility, diligence.

Ask, and ye shall receive; knock, and it shall be opened unto you. Amen.

(Doctrine and Covenants, Section 4)

Letter One

"It's All True!"

Dear Elder [ ],

    I hope you don't mind that I'm typing this letter and not handwriting it. I think handwritten letters are more personal, but my handwriting isn't what it used to be so you probably wouldn't be able to read it.

    I'm sure you are aware that there is a section in the ward newsletter each month devoted to missionary news. It's the first place I look when it is delivered to our home. I thoroughly enjoy reading about our missionaries so I hope your parents will write a few lines in future newsletters telling us about where you are and how you are doing.

    I don't really have any news from the ward to report to you. I'm sure your parents have communicated any news that is noteworthy. I haven't been able to get out to church (or go to work) because I've been laid up at home for the past two or three months and will continue to be so for many more months to come. I have considerable pain in my legs and feet; and my leg muscles have atrophied to nearly nothing so I can't walk without aid. I have also lost 40 lbs. After a battery of tests and visits to multiple doctors, I finally learned that I have a rare neurological illness. Although medical science can do little to help me, the good news is my body will heal itself for the most part. The bad news is the healing process will take up to two years. So I will need to learn patience.

    Since I have an abundance of time on my hands these days, I thought I would make myself useful by writing to you and the other missionaries from our ward. I remember from my own missionary experience (so many years ago) how much missionaries appreciate letters from home. Although I don't know you well personally, I

Inspiration and Healing

know how much my wife loves you. Bonnie, bless her heart, has gone back to work as an office manager in a new audiologist office. She says "hello" and she misses you. We are both proud of you.

Elder [ ], a mission is a succession of good times, difficult times, and plenty of routine times in between. They all combine over the term of your mission to provide you with the greatest experience of your life to date. You will grow in so many ways and your service will touch the lives of many for good as you do your part to grow the kingdom of God on earth. You will always look back on your mission with fondness and as the great turning point of your life. Be strong, yet humble; obey the mission rules; love the people you serve; live close to the Lord; be diligent in the work; and you will be a successful missionary. Do not measure success by baptisms alone; leave that measurement up to the Lord.

Let me tell you a story. Every missionary loves his mission president and I am no exception. I knew my mission president, Royden G. Derrick of Salt Lake City, better than most of the missionaries because I served in the mission office for 9 months as the mission secretary and a little later as his executive secretary to three member districts (which are all stakes now). So we spent a lot of time together, not only in the office, but traveling throughout the mission and the member districts.

Over the years since, we have stayed in touch. Later in his life, he became a General Authority of the Church and was one of the Seven Presidents of the Seventy. He sealed Bonnie and me in the Salt Lake Temple and later ordained me a High Priest in the Melchizedek Priesthood. When the Derrick's returned to Utah and were able to regularly attend our mission reunions, he moved them to the Jordan River Temple (having previously served as president of the Seattle temple).

Elder Derrick passed away a year ago in December having lived well into his 90's. He and his good wife, Allie, were still so fond of "their" missionaries that at his funeral she had all their former missionaries from England and Ireland who were in attendance, and there were many, come to the front of the chapel surrounding his casket and sing the missionary anthem *Ye Elders of Israel* followed by our reciting the Fourth Section of the Doctrine and Covenants. At the next reunion, Sister Derrick said that was the highlight of the funeral service for her.

Let me continue the story. I went early to the LDS stake center in the avenues area of Salt Lake City to go to the viewing before attending President Derrick's funeral service. There was a long line. I barely made it into the relief society room where the family was when the funeral director had to turn people away so they would be able to begin the funeral on time.

It was great joy for me to greet the Derrick family, who I have come to know over the years (their youngest son was with them in England). As I walked toward the casket I noticed the crowd of extended family and close friends gathered there, who had been rather noisy, suddenly grew quiet. I turned to see why and I saw that our revered Thomas S. Monson, the President of the Church, had entered the room. The crowd separated like Moses parting the Red Sea. I stopped in my place because President Monson and I were both moving toward the casket so, of course, I deferred my position to him. He didn't say a word to anyone as he respectfully and quietly walked through the parted crowd and stopped at the casket only a few feet from me. He looked down upon his friend, "Royd," as if reflecting on some of their good times together and of his great service to the Lord and the Church, yet with some sadness at his passing.

After a few moments, he turned to his right to greet the family. There I stood, directly in his path. Instead of moving out of his way as anyone else would have done, I reached out my hand to shake his. What was I thinking? He extended his hand to shake mine, graciously smiled at me, and then gently moved me out of the way with his large hand. What a great day, being part of honoring my beloved mission president and shaking the hand of the Lord's prophet.

I really should end now, but I have one more story in conclusion. Bonnie recently met a man at her employment who had been the

Inspiration and Healing

stake president in Nauvoo when they were planning and then building the new temple there. On one occasion, this brother was meeting with President Faust, who was Second Counselor to President Hinckley in the First Presidency at the time. At the end of their meeting, President Faust asked him to come closer. President Faust then firmly told him that all the knowledge we have in the Church is true. "It's all true!" he said.

I join my own humble testimony with his. God, our Heavenly Father, lives! Joseph Smith was a true prophet who ushered in the restoration of the fullness of the gospel of Jesus Christ to the earth in these last days. The Church is true. President Monson is the Lord's prophet on the earth today. The Book of Mormon is true. It's all true! May God bless you in your worthy work. Until we meet again, I remain........

Your brother in the gospel,

Brother Dewey

Excerpts from Missionary Return Letters

Dear Bro Dewey,

I'm really glad to hear from you. Thank you very much for the letter. It was the first letter I have received in my new area. Thank you so very much for remembering me.

I'm really sorry to hear about your condition. I am sure it must be hard for you. I will include you and your wife in my prayers.

Bro. Dewey, I really want to thank you and your wife for all you have done for me and my family. I remember your wife teaching in Sunday School and how amazingly patient she was and what a calm influence you always were and what a great example you always were.

Your talk about your experience as a missionary and your experience with your Mission President really helped me out. Thank you. You knew just what to say and just what I needed to hear. You have a great command of words and I wish I had that and I wish I had better handwriting so I hope you can read this. Thank you for all you do and I wish you the best in recovery and hope all is well.

Until we meet again may God be with you!
Elder [ ]

Dear Bro. Dewey,

Thank you so much for the letters, words cannot describe how much your letter meant to me! I have been going through a rough time and Heavenly Father has helped me see that I have great support from home and that He is very mindful of me. Thank you again for the letter, I needed it very much.

I am back in [ ]. I am happy that I can do service after the tornado. It was really neat to see the community get together and help each other, it doesn't matter what religion you belong to [when it comes to service].

Bro. Dewey, I'm sorry to hear about your health problems. I wish there was something I could do for you! Learning patience is not very easy, but what a great Christ like attitude it is to develop! Something I have thought a lot about on my mission. I admire you for your good attitude, I don't know if I could handle that as well as you have.

I loved your story about meeting President Monson. That would be awesome to meet him!

Well, Bro. Dewey, I wish my letter was as interesting and helpful as yours was but I am not the best writer. I just want you to know that I greatly appreciate you and your wife's loving support. May God bless you and your family!

Your brother in the gospel,
Elder [ ]

Dear David Dewey,

Thank you so much for writing me. As you probably know, getting mail as a missionary is about the best thing there is!

I'm glad to hear that you're continuing to improve and recover! I'm grateful that you would take the time to write me. Life gets busy at home.

Thank you for sharing your experiences and testimony. You got to shake the prophet's hand? What an incredible man.

I can tell you that the people I meet here will be my life-long friends.

Thanks again for your letter and I hope you are doing well. I'll continue to work my hardest.
Elder [ ]

Letter Two

Inspiration from the Holy Ghost

Dear Elder [ ],

This month in the ward newsletter your parents noted that you have already been in the mission field for a year; my, how time flies. I hope you're enjoying your work training a new elder. I remember the new elder I trained. He had just spent a year at BYU Hawaii – not studying much, mostly surfing, lounging around and tanning on the beach. It took awhile to transition him from that easy going lifestyle to that of a hard working missionary. He turned out to be a great missionary.

Bonnie and I appreciated and enjoyed your letter. It has been years since we have received a letter from a missionary, our daughter. Please know that there is no expectation on my part, and you should feel no obligation on your part, to write to me in return. I fully understand how busy you are on your weekly preparation day - with so much to do and so little time to do it. I'm just pleased that my letters might provide you with some encouragement and perhaps a little inspiration.

I continue to suffer from this crazy neurological disease and haven't noticed any observable improvement, yet my neurologist assures me it will come. In the Book of Mormon, Nephi said he didn't know the meaning of all things but he knew that God loves His children.[15] If you and I can know that, then we can bear up under our afflictions as sons and daughters of God because He knows the end from the beginning and therefore knows what's best for us.

I hope you had the opportunity to enjoy some or all of General Conference earlier this month. In the Priesthood session, Elder W.

Inspiration and Healing

Christopher Waddell made this profound statement that caused me to think of you, "Your mission is a training ground for life. The experiences, lessons, testimony and knowledge, obtained through faithful service are meant to provide a gospel-centered foundation that will last throughout mortality and into the eternities."[16] From my experience, I can say *amen* to that.

One of the things you learn in the mission field is the importance of regular prayer and how to rely on the Lord for answers to your prayers through the inspiration of the Holy Ghost. I was fortunate to have had a mother who taught me this at an early age so it has always been an important part of my life.

Let me tell you a story. A number of years ago, Bonnie and I traveled to Europe to pick up our second daughter from her mission in Slovenia. We spent a week in her mission area and then spent another week traveling in Western Europe ending in Paris, France.

It was important that we not be late for our flight home the next morning so that we wouldn't miss our connecting flight from New York to Salt Lake because, unknown to our daughter, a house full of family and close friends would be there to give her a surprise "welcome home" party.

The next day we got up early to allow plenty of time for us to drive to the airport, return our rental car, and check in at the Delta ticket counter on time. In spite of our plan, we experienced a succession of problems beyond our control, including a downpour of rain, which caused us to arrive late at the terminal. I've traveled quite a lot in my career and have stood in my share of lines in airports, but the line at the Delta counter that morning in Paris was the longest I have ever seen. I was mortified by the distinct possibility that we would not get through the line in time to catch our flight.

There was a security lady standing toward the end of the line who spoke some English. I asked her if she thought we would get through the line in time to make our flight. She said quite matter-of-factly, "No, you are going to have to make other arrangements." I suspected she enjoyed giving us the bad news. If we missed our flight, it would ruin the surprise for our daughter. So I asked my wife and daughter to stay in line while I left for a minute.

The Delta counter was at the end of the large terminal. In the corner was a pillar that was set out from the wall a few feet. I went over there, stood behind the pillar out of sight of everybody, and prayed to Heavenly Father for help. I explained what had happened and while this problem may not be particularly important to Him, it was very important to us, and asked if He would help us and how extremely grateful I would be. When I got back to my family, the line hadn't moved much. My wife asked where I had gone. I told her what I had done.

Just then she noticed a man in a Delta uniform walking back and forth in front of the ticket counter. He appeared to be a supervisor or manager. She said, "Him," pointing to the man. "You need to go talk to him." Somehow I knew she was right, though I didn't want to do it. I am not good at groveling, plus I believe in fairness and it wouldn't be right for us to try to get ahead of all the other people who were waiting in line. My wife saw the grimace in my face but when I saw the look on her face I knew I had no choice.

I walked the long way around to the end of the ticket counter rather than walk up the long line of people and draw attention to myself. I approached the man in the Delta uniform. I was sure he wouldn't speak English and I would be doomed from the beginning. To my surprise, he spoke perfect English. In fact, he was an American working in Paris as part of an employee exchange. With my tail between my legs, I explained our situation. When I was done, he looked at me for a moment without saying a word as if he was "sizing me up." The look on his face suggested that he had heard many such sad stories and he would not be able to help us. Then he surprised me again when he said, "Wait here" and hurriedly disappeared behind the ticket counter. I'm sure he was gone for only a couple of minutes, yet it seemed like an eternity. I offered another silent prayer that he would be able to help us.

He came back with a new ticket agent and put her in an empty station at the end of the counter. He said, "Hurry, get your family

Inspiration and Healing

up here and this agent will help you with your tickets and I'll help you check your bags." I signaled to my wife and daughter to join us. We all worked feverishly. He got on his hand-held radio and spoke to someone in French. When we were done, he said, "Follow me, quickly." We walked briskly behind him to where more people were waiting in lines for their security screenings. At the far end was a station reserved for the handicapped and persons in wheelchairs. There was no one in that line, so he took us to that station and we rushed through. On the other side, I learned why he had called on his radio. He had summoned a cart and driver to drive us to our gate. He wished us well and we thanked him profusely. We arrived at the gate and were the last passengers to board the airplane. After stowing our carry-on bags, we took our seats, took a breath and offered silent prayers of thanks for divine intervention in our time of need.

Many times, if we are in tune, the Holy Ghost inspires us to do such things that we might be the means of answering the prayers of others. Another short story is in order. Many years ago, I was driving home from work one day and was within a few miles of home when I felt the impression to turn into a small strip mall and go to the video rental store there. We occasionally rented movies at that location, but I didn't know of any reason why I should go there at that moment so I shrugged off the impression. Then the impression came again, even stronger than before, so I immediately responded by turning into the strip mall and parking in front of the video store. I got out of the car and walked into the store. Once inside, I stopped and wondered why I was there.

I looked around and didn't see anyone I knew or didn't observe anyone in need. So I walked up and down a couple of the isles of movies ending up at the far end of store. There I saw someone I recognized, a man from our ward with his three small children. He looked a little frazzled. "Bill," I said, "How are you doing?" Bill explained that had been driving his kids home when his car broke down. He had come across the street into the video store to use their phone to call for help (this was before cell phones). He found that his wife wasn't home from work yet and the neighbors he called weren't home either. His kids were getting hungry and fussy and he didn't know what to do. *Now* I knew why I was there. I said, "Let me take you and your children home. I'm on the way to the neighborhood right now. Let's go."

He responded, "But you haven't rented your video yet."

"That's OK," I said. "I didn't really want one anyway,"

As we walked out to the car, he thanked me and said I was an answer to his prayer.

Now that wasn't a big thing to me, but to him it was important so he prayed for help. The Lord looked around and saw me nearby so He sent the Holy Ghost to direct me to his rescue. Isn't it great how God works?

Well, those are enough stories for this time. I hope you're enjoying your mission. I know your testimony of the truthfulness of the Gospel is growing. One of the primary purposes of our mortal probation is to help our fellow brothers and sisters in any way we can since we are all on this journey together. And what better service can we provide than to teach them the way to obtain salvation and eternal life as families in the presence of Heavenly Father, through Jesus Christ, our Lord. Harder said than done, I know, but worth every effort we can muster. With the help of God, all things are possible.

May God bless you in your worthy work. It's all true! Until we meet again, I remain……..

Your brother in the gospel,

Brother Dewey

Excerpts from Missionary Return Letters

Dave Dewey,

I have to say I love getting your letters. They're always uplifting spiritually and emotionally. I'm glad you're getting better, even if the recovery is slow.

I actually remember the story about your daughter coming home. It's humbling and comforting to know that prayers that aren't necessarily huge needs or something that is not "life or death," and they're still answered.

We have an investigator who already has a huge testimony of prayer. We do what we call prayer contacting. We say that we're representatives of Jesus Christ and offer to bless their homes. She is one of the people we met that way. She told us her friend was sick and a few other needs. Then we blessed her home. When we came back a few days later she told us that her friend was better. She had a tumor or something in her side that was causing her a lot of pain so the doctor wanted to do surgery. She went to another doctor for a second opinion and it was gone. So she realized this was an answer to the prayer.

I hope you are continuing to improve and both you and Bonnie are in my prayers.

Sister [ ]

Dear Bro. and Sis. Dewey,

Thanks so much for writing me, I love hearing about your awesome experiences! I got your package the other day, in fact, it came on my birthday! Thank you for the goodies and the nice letter, Sis. Dewey! I appreciate you both very much and I hope you know that I love you!

Bro. Dewey, I really enjoyed your story about the airport and how you and your wife and daughter were blessed to catch your flight. That was quite the story, it goes to show to always pray and put your trust in Heavenly Father, and to listen to your wife.

The gospel is true and I am grateful to be part of it! I am grateful to you both very much and appreciate your loving support, Bro. Dewey. I hope you will improve soon, always remember that through Christ our burdens may be light. I love you both very much.

Love, Elder [ ]

Letter Three

God is Looking Over You and His Work

Dear Elder [ ],

We learned in the ward newsletter that you are training a new missionary, which says something about the faith and trust your Mission President has in you. I'm sure you recall from your own experience as a new missionary how important a missionary's first companion is for training and setting the tone for the rest of your mission. You will do a great job with your new companion.

I have some good news to report. I've experienced the first sign of improvement in my health in the form of a little more strength and control in my left leg. Ye ha! Thank heaven for the Lord's tender mercies that give us comfort and hope.

I know assuredly that the Lord looks over His great work. I am reminded of a story I heard in the mission field. I don't recall the source so I cannot confirm its authenticity, but it makes a point.

When the Empire of Japan attacked the United States Naval Base at Pearl Harbor, Hawaii, on December 7, 1941, they sent two waves of warplanes. Previous to the attack the Japanese had spies at Pearl Harbor so they knew exactly where our ships and other targets were located. Many of the pilots had been given specific targets to bomb, torpedo and strafe. After the ships in the harbor had been mostly destroyed, other pilots flew over the island to attack airfields and important buildings.

More than thirty years later, when I was on my mission in England, a couple of elders reportedly tracted out an older Japanese man. Back in those days we all carried homemade "flip charts" while tracting so we could visually support whatever verbal door approach we had chosen. On this particular occasion, the elder flipped to a page showing several pictures of temples that were operating in the Church at that time. The man listened politely for a few moments then interrupted the missionary by pointing to the picture of the temples and inquired about it.

The elder said they were pictures of some of the temples in our Church that we revere as sacred edifices. The man specifically pointed to the picture of the Hawaiian Temple and asked where it was located. The elder said that it was in Hawaii. Then the man told this story.

He said he had piloted one of the airplanes that attacked Pearl Harbor. As he flew over the northern part of the island, he saw the building pictured in the missionary's flipchart. It looked very impressive and important so he decided to destroy it by strafing it with his machine guns and dropping a bomb on it. But when he tried to fire the guns, they wouldn't fire; and when he tried to release the bomb, it failed to release. He could not believe they had both jammed. As he flew back south across the island, he tried attacking another target. This time his guns fired normally and his bomb released perfectly. He said he had often wondered about that building. Now, after all these years, he finally understood what it was and why he could not destroy it. He said they have temples in his Buddhist religion which they also hold sacred.

Likewise, God is looking over you and the work you are doing as a missionary. Of all the missions in the world, you were assigned to your specific mission by inspiration from the Lord.

Some years ago I worked with a fellow whose uncle was a member of the Quorum of the Seventy. My co-worker had a daughter who decided to serve a full-time mission. She suffered from juvenile arthritis that was made worse by cold weather, so when they submitted her missionary application papers they requested that she serve in a warm climate. Wouldn't you know it; she was called to serve in Minnesota, one of the coldest states in the country. Understandably, her mother was quite concerned by this and called her husband's uncle in the Seventy to see if he might do something about it. He referred her to the missionary committee of the Church where she was able to speak with a member of the

Quorum of the Twelve Apostles. He graciously explained to her that her daughter had been called to Minnesota by inspiration from the Lord and that is where she needed to serve.

Not long after arriving in Minnesota, the sister missionary became acquainted with a member of the Church who was a doctor at the Mayo Clinic, which is a world renowned medical practice and research hospital specializing in treating difficult patients. He happened to be one of the country's foremost experts on juvenile arthritis and he agreed to treat her while she was on her mission, at no cost. As a result of his care, she felt better during her mission than she had felt before she left home and was able to serve a successful mission in good health.

Elder [ ], you are where you are for a reason, called by inspiration from on high. There are people there you need to meet who specifically need your personal touch, your manner of teaching, your spirit, your testimony and your love.

Thank you for being such a great example to everybody who knows you. Your faithful service in the mission field is not only important for building up the kingdom of God on earth, but you will help inspire others who look up to you. Your service also blesses your family and all who support you in every way, including Bonnie and me. And finally, your missionary service will be one of the greatest blessings to you in your entire life.

May God continue to bless you, inspire you, and protect you in performing His work. It's all true! As always, I remain……..

Your brother in the gospel,

Brother Dewey

Excerpts from Missionary Return Letters

Dear Brother Dewey,
I wanted to let you know how much I appreciate your letters.
The stories you've shared are inspiring and always remind me

Inspiration and Healing

of the importance and sacredness of this work. You mentioned in your last letter about how the missionaries used to use "flip charts." I think we need those back for this area! Most people here are very visual learners and we've seen more success using pictures and object lessons than anything else.

I'm really grateful for the content and timing of your last letter. At times it's easy to wonder if our work here is making any difference whatsoever. I loved what you said about God calling us to where we need to be. There's been so much I've learned and realized here that I couldn't have learned anywhere else in the world. I'm truly loving my time here.

I look forward to your inspiring words. Thanks again!
Elder [ ]

Brother Dewey,
    Hey! Thank you so much for writing me.
    Thank you so much for your words of encouragement. They mean so much and I enjoy hearing from you.
    Sincerely,
Elder [ ]

Letter Four

Living Prophets

Dear Elder [ ],

I hope this letter arrives in a timely manner. We were pleased to receive your colorful and cleverly folded "note." You expressed appreciation to us for our letters. Thank you, but it is *we* who appreciate *you* and your faithful service. We find joy in supporting you in some small way.

In the annual First Presidency Christmas fireside last weekend, it was mentioned how we should remember to put Christ back into Christmas. I recall how that was our theme for the two Christmas's I spent in the mission field. I'm sure you are doing the same.

Today I want to testify of the divine validity of modern prophets. The prophets guide this great Church under the direction of Jesus Christ. They love us. They warn us away from the pitfalls of the world and then direct us toward the things that will bring us true joy in this life and in the life to come.

Some years ago, my father-in-law and I served for several years as ushers at the venerable and historic tabernacle on Temple Square in downtown Salt Lake City. While we primarily worked during the semi-annual General Conference sessions of the Church, we also worked other performances, meetings and activities that were held at the tabernacle. The tabernacle was divided into five usher sections. We worked in the fifth section on the west end, which included the stand, General Authority seating and choir areas. It was easy duty compared to the other sections. In fact, the only challenging time was when visiting choirs came to sing. After sessions of conference they tended to want to come down into the areas under the choir seats, behind where the General Authorities are seated which is "off limits" to them. We had instructions to kindly restrain them, especially until after the General Authorities had left the building. Basically the only persons allowed in our area were the General Authorities, Church security officers, ushers and occasionally Church operations personnel (who were primarily maintenance and custodial people). To properly identify these approved persons, each wore lapel pins that were specific to their group (except General Authorities). If someone was found wandering around without a proper lapel pin, we knew they did not belong there and they were kindly escorted away to where they should be.

On one occasion, at the end of a session of conference during the administration of President Ezra Taft Benson, we were restraining a guest choir to allow the General Authorities to exit the building. At that moment, a young man from the operations department walked out of the restroom having just replenished its supplies. I asked him to stand with me for a few minutes while the Authorities passed. Just then President and Sister Benson, along with his personal secretary and his security officer, were walking past us toward the elevator. Suddenly, President Benson stopped right in front of the young custodian standing next to me, shook his hand and asked, "Where are you going on your mission?"

The surprised young man responded, "I don't know. I'm waiting for my mission call right now."

"Oh, that's wonderful," exclaimed President Benson with a big smile on his face. "I wish I was going with you."

Afterward, I asked the young man if he knew President Benson, since he was the only person the prophet stopped to talk to and he seemed to pick him out of the small crowd as if he recognized him. He said, "No, I've never met him. I can't believe how he knew I was going on a mission."

I suggested that he should always remember that day and if he ever had any problems with any of his companions he should tell them, "The prophet wanted to be my companion."

Some years later, toward the end of President Spencer W. Kimball's life and tenure as president of the Church, his health was failing so he wasn't able to attend General Conference very often. Occasionally, he was brought to one of the sessions of conference although he was unable to deliver a speech. It saddened me to watch him at that time during his poor health and advanced age after he had lived such a robust life and had led the Church so admirably during challenging times.

I think it might have been the last time he was brought to conference, I was standing in my assigned ushering area before the start of one of the sessions of General Conference when the elevator door opened and out came President Kimball being pushed in a wheelchair by his security officer. It was unusual that there were no other persons with them. After exiting the elevator, they stopped and the security officer signaled me to follow them. He pushed the president's chair to the right into an empty room. I followed them into the room. The security officer asked me to stay with the president for a few minutes while he went to make some arrangements. He left and closed the door behind him.

There I stood in that silent room alone with the prophet of the Lord. President Kimball was slightly bent over at the waist with his head down. He appeared to be asleep. You can only try to imagine the feeling of awesome reverence I had at that moment. I just stood there, like a statue, at his right side, looking straight ahead, not knowing if I dared turn my head to gaze upon him. I took a peek at him and then looked straight again. Just then I noticed him move so I looked toward him again. He rose up in his chair and turned his head to see me as best he could. He raised his right hand and gently grasped my left arm which hung down at my side. Then, in his signature raspy voice, he quietly uttered the words, "I love you." After which he slowly returned to his former posture.

Elder [ ], at that moment, my testimony of a living prophet felt like electricity surging through my body. My heart swelled with joy. "Men are that they might have joy."[17] We cannot begin to imagine the fullness of joy we will feel when, if we have lived worthily and endured to the end, we will meet our Lord and Savior, Jesus Christ, in the next life and He will say, "Well done, thou good and faithful servant."[18] I love you.

Yours is a message of joy; joy that may be in this life as well as in the life to come. Two thousand years ago, a God was made mortal. He said, come follow me and I will show you the way. The way is straight and narrow and few there be that find it.[19] He is our Savior, the Redeemer of the world, and the only way by which mankind may be saved.

Bonnie and I extend to you a heartfelt Merry Christmas! May God continue to bless you as you are engaged in His work, putting Christ back into Christmas. It's all true! As always, I remain……..

Your brother in the gospel,

Brother Dewey

Excerpts from Missionary Return Letters

Dear Brother Dewey,

Thank you so much for your recent letters. Yours are always the most spiritual and uplifting. I hope you had a Merry Christmas and are having a happy New Year!

Thank you for sharing your experience with one of God's prophets in your last letter. I was deeply touched as it strengthened my own testimony of the divinity of God's chosen servants.

I want to share a spiritual experience I had the other day. A few nights ago before going to bed my companion said our nightly companionship prayer. Both he and I will be completing our missions this year. In his prayer he thanked God for the New Year and for the chance that he and I would have to serve Him for part of it. I knew what he meant, however, as he said those words I instantly thought to myself, "I'm going to serve Him all of it." You don't have to wear a name tag or knock on doors all day to be in the full time service of our Lord.

I know this to be true and pray that we can all be representatives of Christ throughout this New Year and [all of]

our lives.
Your brother in the gospel,
Elder [ ]

Dear Brother Dewey,
Thank you for that uplifting letter. I really loved that story about the boy going on a mission and the Prophet telling him that he wanted to be his companion.

I am having the time of my life. It's crazy being here. I just hope that I can be a blessing to those I have been called to serve.

Thanks for your inspiring advice. I hope to always be able to have a strong testimony of the prophet. I know that President Monson is called of God. Thanks again for everything.

Love,
Elder [ ]

Letter Five

Selfless Service

Dear Elder [ ],

Thank you so much for your letter and your Christmas card. Sister Dewey and I enjoy hearing from you and how you are doing. It is abundantly clear that you have experienced tremendous growth on your mission. Please know that we have no expectation for you to reply to each of my letters. We completely understand how busy you are and we don't want to be a distraction from your work or from the multitude of tasks you need to do on your preparation day.

I'm sure it was difficult being away from home on Christmas, and I know everyone at home misses you, however there is nothing better that you could be doing right now than serving the Lord in the mission field and forgetting about yourself. I recently finished a new book by Elder Dallin H. Oaks wherein he spoke about unselfish service:

"Shortly after my calling as an Apostle I had a landmark lesson about the deficiency of service that is conscious of self. I spoke with Elder Boyd K. Packer about how inadequate I felt for the calling I had received. He responded with this mild reproof and challenging insight:

"'I suppose your feelings are understandable. But you should work for a condition where you will not be preoccupied by yourself and your own feelings of inadequacy and can give your entire concern to others and to the work of the Lord in all the world.'"[20]

Understandably, the transition from being who you were and what you were doing before your mission, to becoming a selfless missionary in the service of the Lord takes some doing. Elder Oaks addressed his own experience with this matter as well:

"I had time for deep reflection on the responsibilities I would soon assume and exercise for the rest of my life. I felt very inadequate and very apprehensive. I took an inventory of my professional credentials, experience, and qualifications and compared them with the kinds of things I thought I would be called upon to do as an Apostle. I asked myself, 'Throughout the remainder of my life, will you be a lawyer and judge who has been called to be an Apostle, or will you be an Apostle who used to be a lawyer and judge?'

"There is a tendency in most of us to spend most of our time doing what we feel comfortable in doing – to seek to fulfill responsibilities through activities in which we feel a sense of mastery or at least familiarity. I knew I must not surrender to that tendency.

"The most important parts of my new calling – the only parts really unique in the service of the Lord – were those parts that I know nothing about, the parts where I would have to start all over at the beginning. I knew that if I concentrated my time on the things that came naturally – the things that I felt qualified to do – I would never measure up as an Apostle. I decided I would focus my efforts on becoming what I had been called to be, not on what I felt qualified to do. I determined that instead of trying to shape my calling to my credentials, I would try to shape myself to my calling."[21]

Wise counsel, I believe, for anyone engaged in the service of the Lord.

During the first several months of my mission (which seems like a lifetime ago, yet only yesterday), I served as a junior companion to three district leaders in two areas. Each was a tremendous learning experience for me. After about six months I was transferred to a new area as a senior companion. My junior companion had been out for nineteen months. What is wrong with this picture?

This elder had not made the transition from being what he was before his mission to shaping himself to the calling of a missionary. The mission rules and programs meant little to him. He wanted to do the work his way. I'll spare you the horrid details of what turned out to be the most severe challenge of my mission, but I will share one relevant story.

My new companion did not believe in door-to-door contacting and often refused to go out. On one particular day, somehow I got him to go out tracting with me. I hoped we would have a good experience for his sake. Unfortunately, few people were at home and those who were home were not interested in hearing our message. My companion noticed a cloud in the sky off in the distance that appeared to be moving our way. He pointed out the "raincloud" and reminded me that he absolutely refused to tract in the rain. He announced that he was going to the bus stop to catch the next bus back to our flat, with or without me.

Of course, I couldn't continue working without my companion, nor could I force him to stay out with me (which would be Satan's way) and I didn't want to go in early. As a new senior companion I didn't know what to do, but recognized this was a decisive moment. Fortunately, the Lord saw my plight and intervened. I suddenly felt a surge of inspiration from the Holy Ghost. Words flowed from my mouth before I consciously knew what I was saying. I told my companion that if he would stay out with me and tract one more street, I *promised* him that we would find someone who would let us in and hear our message. He looked at me with surprise and suspicion, but he agreed. I could tell he was testing me and would never let me forget it if I was wrong.

After knocking on three or four doors, a young mother with two small children finally opened her door to us. She said she would normally be at work at this time of day, but her young daughter was sick so she had stayed home to care for her. We learned that she was recently divorced and was now a single mom feeling a nearly overwhelming weight of responsibility for home, kids, work and her own needs. She was very stressed out and had been wondering what life was really all about and if there was a better way to live. She invited us into her home hoping that we might have some answers for her. You should have seen the look on my companion's face, it was priceless.

Elder [ ], may God continue to love and keep you. I testify that "it's all true!" As always, I remain……..

Your brother in the gospel,

Brother Dewey

Excerpts from Missionary Return Letters

Dear Brother Dewey,

I cannot thank you enough for the letters [you have] sent me. Every single one of your letters has inspired and uplifted me. Your letters are and <u>will</u> be very cherished for the rest of my life. I would first like to tell you about [one] of your letters that has, in particular, helped me.

In February you shared with me a portion of Dallin H. Oaks's book. I decided I would focus my efforts on becoming what I had been called to be, not on what I felt qualified to do. I determined that instead of trying to shape my calling to my credentials, I would try to shape myself to my calling. Wise words. A lot of time we do not understand or realize our potential. When I first read that letter I did not see my own potential. After I read your letter I realized the Lord knows I have great potential as a missionary. I now must forget everything else and live up to my potential as a worker in the Lord's vineyard. Ever since I have tried to live up to my true potential!

I love this work, Brother Dewey, and I know that each of us can reach our God-given potential through faith in his Son and in the Book of Mormon.

"It's all true" and I remain your brother in the Gospel, Elder [ ]

Letter Six

Inspired Mission Presidents

Dear Elder [ ],

It is hard to believe another month has passed. Elder [ ] has returned from his mission. Unfortunately, he was ill on the day he was scheduled to speak in Church so his report has been rescheduled for later this month. Elder [ ] is out of the Mission Training Center and now laboring in Argentina. Also we had Elder Dallin H. Oaks speak at the Saturday night adult session of our Stake Conference. He has a much greater sense of humor than you might expect.

In my last letter, I wrote about an experience I had with a "challenging" companion from my own mission days who struggled with following the program and living the mission rules. I just finished reading a short book by a former missionary, Brother Bob Lonsberry, who served on and around the Indian reservations of the American Southwest. He developed a wonderful attitude regarding his companions which I would like to share with you:

"There are all kinds of guys out there. Some of them will rub you the wrong way. But I always figured I probably rubbed them the wrong way, too. I haven't met a perfect missionary, yet. But I haven't met anybody I couldn't work with.

"What is going to be is going to be. And I think in life you've got to realize that when the Lord blesses you it isn't always fun. I figure whoever I get put with, it's the Lord's will and he does things for a reason. I might not always understand that reason, but it's always there and I've got to have faith in that. And my obligation is always the same. I've got to work hard, love the people, help my companion and live up to my calling.

"And my companion's got to do the same thing. He and I might be different in certain ways, but we're both missionaries, we're both children of God, we're both members of the Church. I think we can work anything out, we can get through anything. And remember, you're not supposed to *endure* your companion, you're supposed to *uplift* him. Maybe the soul you were sent out here to save is your companion. Maybe the soul he was sent out to save is you."[22]

It's true; the Lord does things for a reason. Your mission president is inspired of the Lord and you can have confidence in him as he makes companionship changes. The Lord blesses and protects him. Speaking of that divine protection, I am reminded of an experience I had with my mission president that profoundly established this point for me.

At the time, I was serving in the mission office as the mission secretary and the executive secretary to the mission president for our three member districts. As such, I worked closely with the mission president and often traveled around the mission with him. One Sunday I accompanied him for a full schedule of meetings associated with a district conference. After which, the president conducted interviews with several members. It was well into the evening before we were finally able to start our drive back to the mission home, a trip of about one and a half hours. The president asked me if I would be willing to drive so he might stretch out on the back seat and get some rest. Although I, too, was tired, I was happy to accommodate his request.

After about an hour of driving, I caught myself nearly dozing off a couple of times. I did everything I could think of to stay awake. The president lay asleep on the back seat. We had just merged on to the ring road around the last city before reaching our home town. There are many "roundabouts" (or circles) on the roads of England and I knew from making the trip several times before that we were soon approaching two large ones. Roundabouts have to be carefully negotiated in order to avoid crashing into other vehicles entering and exiting while making sure you take the correct exit. I remembered seeing the first roundabout directly ahead. The next thing I remembered we had just exited out of the second one. You can't imagine the shock and horror I felt knowing I must have been asleep at the wheel during that entire section of road and somehow successfully navigated two major roundabouts. I might have easily gotten into an accident and killed my mission president, forget about my own life. There is no question that a greater power had taken control of our car during that stretch of road in order to protect a faithful mission president who would later serve as a temple president and a General Authority of the Church.

Full time missionary service is both challenging and amazingly rewarding. Only those who have served a mission can really understand what you are experiencing. I think Brother Lonsberry said it very well:

"This is a roll-up-your-sleeves gospel, and the calling of a missionary is to work. Sure, there is praying and reading and pondering to be done, but preaching and reading and pondering the gospel is primarily a calling of toil. The Lord sent His disciples out into the world to labor and counseled them in modern times to thrust in their sickles with their might. It's one of those things where if you're not tired, you're not doing it right. If it's not using up everything you have to give, you need to do it better.

"Because a mission is hard. It's lump-in-your-throat, tears-in-your-eyes hard. Anybody who thinks the 'best two years of your life' come easy or free is nuts. Every good thing comes at a cost, and this is the best good thing. This is walking where Jesus walked, this is doing what Jesus did, this is bearing what Jesus bore. And while he doesn't ask his disciples to follow him into the garden or onto the cross, he does ask them to watch and wait and to share in his labors. And that is soul-building hard. And it doesn't let up until the stake president tells you you're released and your mom takes the name tag from your jacket and you go on to the next set of responsibilities."[23]

Elder [ ], may God continue bless you in your discipleship. And remember to have some fun too. I testify that it's all true! As always, I remain……..

Your brother in the gospel,

Brother Dewey

Excerpts from Missionary Return Letters

Dear Brother Dewey,
    Thank you so much for writing me. You must be pretty inspired when you write because every letter seems to apply so well to where I am at the time.
    My biggest fear as a missionary is that I won't be able to do everything Heavenly Father sent me to do. I have been serving very hard to <u>become</u> the missionary He knows I can be and as you said in your letter that can be very hard. I think I have made some progress but I still have a long way to go.
    I have the best Mission President. I have so much confidence in him and his calling that I know whatever happens is inspired.
    How is the healing process going? Again thank you so much for writing it really means a lot to me.
    Love,
Sister [ ]

Letter Seven

A Missionary's Sacrifice

Dear Sister [ ],

We received your letter and were surprised to hear about your transfer. Your ability to embrace change is a great blessing which will serve you well in all areas of your life. Few people handle change well. You have such a wonderful attitude which is inspiring to us. I trust this new area will be good to you.

This past Sunday, Elder [ ] and his younger brother brought the sacrament to me at home. What a delight it was for Bonnie and me to talk to Elder [ ] about his mission and learn that his brother has started preparing his missionary application papers.

I have often thought of the sacrifice that it takes to serve a full-time mission and I marvel at the willingness of a young person, like you, to make that sacrifice. I just finished reading a great book by Elder C. Max Caldwell, a former member of the Quorum of the Seventy, who encapsulated the meaning and importance of the law of sacrifice so well that I thought I would share some of it with you because it speaks well of your service.

After the Lord's atoning sacrifice, the ancient Mosaic law was fulfilled and replaced by the higher law of "a sacrifice unto me of a broken heart and contrite spirit," and if they "are willing to observe their covenants by sacrifice – yea, every sacrifice which I, the Lord, shall command – they are accepted of me.

"A willing sacrifice of all earthly things is prerequisite to obtaining the power from on high that results in a faith in Christ unto salvation. If we want to increase our faith, we must acquire and develop a willingness to sacrifice all earthly things. Earthly or worldly things can take many obvious forms, such as money, vehicles, houses, clothes, music, movies, etc. Other more subtle examples might include activities, styles, philosophies, time, interests, and attitudes.

"One great example of a person sacrificing earthly things is a missionary. Everything just mentioned is part of a missionary's experience. Money that would have been earned by staying home and being employed – not to mention the money spent during the mission experience – is an earthly thing. The time given to the calling is earthly. Music, television, movies, cars, and stylish clothes are earthly things one does without. Athletics and personal interests are set aside. All of these things are discarded by missionaries that they might have greater faith and work more closely with the Holy Spirit in the Lord's work. Missionaries need spiritual power, and they acquire it as they remove barriers to their sacred and concentrated focus on the Lord. The Church has guided and assisted missionaries to implement this principle by setting mission standards for them to follow.

"There are three categories or different ways by which we observe the law of sacrifice: (1) sacrifice of all earthly things, (2) giving away our sins, and (3) denial of self.

"Missionaries fit all three dimensions of the law of sacrifice. A true missionary is willing to give up all earthly things to serve the Lord on a mission. Secondly, interviews with the bishop and stake president help determine if there has been a sacrifice of sin or unrighteousness. Third, a missionary is called to serve someone else. Certainly there are many personal benefits from the service, but that is not the motive. The purpose in serving is to share the gospel with others."[24]

Sister [ ], I acknowledge your worthy sacrifice as a servant of the Lord doing His work in the service of others.

Recently, President Monson asked Church members to reread the Book of Mormon this year, especially since we are studying it in the Gospel Doctrine class in Sunday School. I started reading it late last year and finished in January. It's amazing how each time we read that great book, it means more and different things to us because we read it with new eyes and a new heart based on our current life circumstances and having had new experiences since the last reading. This time I came away with a renewed testimony of how much the Book of Mormon truly is, as it says on its cover, another testament of Jesus Christ. And I learned much more about how to be a better disciple of Christ.

I was touched again at the final words of Moroni, in his loneliness and solitude, who was addressing us in our own day, and his brethren the Lamanites, saying "somewhat as seemeth me good." To "all the ends of the earth" he spoke to our time about how the words he had written were true and would come forth "like as one crying from the dead, yea even as one speaking out of the dust." He said, "awake,…and put on thy beautiful garments…of Zion; and strengthen thy stakes and enlarge thy borders forever, that thy covenants of the Eternal Father which he had made unto thee,… may be fulfilled." "Yea, come unto Christ and be perfected in him…"[25]

We are privileged and blessed to have been born in a time and place when and where the restored gospel of Jesus Christ is on the earth. Your goodly parents saw to it that you were taught accordingly so that you might partake of the covenants and the blessings appertaining to His gospel. And now you are respecting and observing your covenants by taking that gospel to Heavenly Father's children, your fellow brothers and sisters, throughout the world. I honor you for your faithful service.

Sister [ ], may God continue to bless you in your selfless service. I believe your sacrifice is accepted of the Lord. I testify that it's all true! As always, I remain…….

Your brother in the gospel,

Brother Dewey

Excerpts from Missionary Return Letters

Dear Brother Dewey,
I just love your letters so much! It really means a lot to me

that you never miss a month and I am grateful for your wonderful example. It would be very easy to justify using your time to pursue worldly things but instead you read uplifting books and write missionaries. I'm also very grateful that you are so in tune with the Spirit. Every letter you send fits perfect with where I am.

Last week was one of the best weeks I've had so far on my mission. It's nice to say when you leave an area, "I've done all I can with the time I was given." And notice a change for the better in yourself and the area. I will miss my companion. I love change!

Thank you again for all you do for me and the Lord's work. I am grateful for the time I have to serve the Lord. I love the gospel so much and the peace and happiness it brings into our lives.

May God bless and keep you.
Sister [ ]

Dear Bro. and Sis. Dewey,
It always brightens the day when you send mail.

It has been really great to be out here on my mission and being a trainer causes me to reflect back constantly to when I was being trained and how much I've grown out here. It has been awesome to see the change.

I can honestly say this has probably been the best year so far in my life which is weird because I've faced constant rejection; terrible days and biting dogs like all the time; but to see myself change and those I teach makes it all worth it. The Church is true and the Book or Mormon is the word of God and it will change the lives of all who read it.

Your friend and Brother,
Elder [ ]

Letter Eight

The Restoration of the Gospel

Dear Sister [ ],

I understand from your parents that you have been experiencing some challenging times lately for reasons beyond your control. Believe me when I tell you, from my own experience, that you will survive and the challenges will only make you stronger. And your mission president has great confidence and trust in you to make you a trainer to a new missionary. You'll be great and you will grow a great deal from the experience.

I hope you had an opportunity to watch much of the General Conference we just experienced. It is always a great spiritual boost and motivates us to greater heights.

Last month I spoke somewhat concerning the sacrifice it takes to serve a full-time mission and I marvel at the willingness of young people, like you, to make that sacrifice. Recently I watched a cable program on BYUtv highlighting a young man who had a promising career ahead of him as a professional baseball player. As he was trying to make the decision about whether or not to serve a mission, he read the following scripture: "And now, behold, I say unto you, that the thing which will be of the most worth unto you will be to declare repentance unto this people, that you may bring souls unto me, that you may rest with them in the kingdom of my Father." (D&C 16:6) He said the spirit really hit him when he read this passage and he was hooked on the idea of not only bringing souls unto Christ, but then being able to be with them into the eternities. He made the decision to serve a mission not knowing whether or not he would still have a baseball career upon his return. He served a great mission, which he has never regretted, and has since been able to pursue a baseball career as well. He knows he has been greatly blessed by the Lord for his decision.

And so it will be with you. Your service as a missionary will bless you and those you have touched forever.

Indeed, as the Lord said, you are there to declare repentance unto this people, that you might bring souls unto God. And what a great place to start teaching people than from "Lesson 1: The Restoration" as outlined in *Preach My Gospel*.[26] The First Vision of the Father and the Son received by the boy prophet, Joseph Smith, in the sacred grove was the culmination of centuries of world preparation the Lord made through the apostasy and the founding of the nation of America in the Promised Land. The story of the First Vision is controversial for some and difficult to believe for others but we do not back down from telling this remarkable truth to the world. It is too important to keep to ourselves. It is meant for the entire world to hear.

I am reminded of the time I was on a business trip to New Jersey. When my business was completed, I took the opportunity to drive to upstate New York to spend a couple of days in the Palmyra area to attend the Hill Cumorah Pageant and visit the other Church historical sites in that vicinity. Perhaps you have been there.

I well remember walking into the sacred grove behind the replica of the Smith family log cabin. I felt awestruck to know I was walking in the same place where Joseph had walked and where the Father and the Son had actually come to earth and appeared to him. I wandered deep into the woods and took in the ambiance of that sacred place. Finally, I found a bench, out of sight of other people, sat down and offered a prayer of thanks to God for what had transpired there. It was a beautiful moment that I will never forget; a time when my testimony was strengthened.

Several years later, while on another business trip, I had the opportunity to spend a couple of days in Kirtland, Ohio, to visit the temple and the other Church history sites in that area. As you probably know, the Kirtland temple is owned by the Community of Christ Church (formerly known as the Reorganized Church of Jesus Christ of Latter-day Saints). The temple tour started in a room in the rear of a small gift shop next to the temple where their tour guide spoke to the small group of tourists for a few minutes and then showed a short film about their church. The film briefly portrays the story of the First Vision from their perspective. It said that Joseph Smith went into the grove of trees to pray and there he had a "spiritual experience." Imagine my surprise and shock to hear that they had reduced the grandeur and eternal significance of the First Vision to a mere spiritual experience. Apparently they are uncomfortable dealing with the difficulty that some may have with the reality of the First Vision. I suppose I shouldn't be critical but I was reminded of what Brigham Young said of Joseph Smith, "I feel like shouting Hallelujah, all the time, when I think that I ever knew Joseph Smith, the Prophet whom the Lord raised up and ordained, and to whom he gave keys and power to build up the Kingdom of God on earth and sustain it."[27]

Sister [ ], I testify to you, with all the fiber of my being, that it's all true! The Father and the Son are real and they love us and have a great plan for us. They did actually appear to the boy prophet as he said they did. Joseph Smith was one of the "noble and great ones"[28] who was chosen before the world was, to be the instrument of the restoration of the true gospel of Jesus Christ in these latter days. The Book of Mormon he brought forth to the world is true. The Church of Jesus Christ of Latter-day Saints is the only true and living Church on the face of the earth. The truth of these things has been revealed to me by the Holy Ghost. And anyone can know these truths in the same way, as Moroni tells us[29], and as you teach to your investigators.

As always, I remain.......
Your brother in the gospel,

Brother Dewey

Excerpts from Missionary Return Letters

Dear Bonnie and Brother Dewey,

I love it here. There are so many cute little kids that want me to play with them or read to them. They are always trying to climb in my lap and then they look so sad when you have to move them. I'm happy to serve wherever Heavenly Father wants me to. He has given me so many blessings that I could never repay Him.

I'm grateful it's Mother's Day on Sunday. By the way, Happy Mother's Day Bonnie! Thank you for always being such a good example to me. You are a great second "mom."

Thank you so much for all your love and support!

Love,
Sister [ ]

Letter Nine

You are Where You are For a Reason

Dear Elder [ ],

    We were so sorry to hear that you had to endure another bout with those blasted kidney stones. What a pain for you, literally as well as figuratively. We appreciate the great work you're doing, even with all of its challenges. You are touching the lives of those who listen to you for good and it is making you a better person.

    There has been an explosion of mission calls received by young members of our ward lately. You have probably already learned that [ ] received his mission call to Michigan; [ ] will be going to Paraguay; and [ ] will be serving in Chili. And last week we learned that [ ] received her call to Arizona - Spanish speaking.

    Sometimes, when considering the immensity of God's creations and His all-powerful dominion over the entire universe and beyond, we may be tempted to fall into a feeling of forlorn that we are only miniscule specks. We might begin to believe that we are insignificant by comparison and, therefore, unimportant and unknown to God. This, of course, is untrue and is one of the devil's tricks to distance us from our Father in Heaven. We know that we are individually very important to our Father and have been from the beginning. In fact, He has specifically prepared each of us and sent us to earth at this particular time to do a work consistent with our specific abilities. Brother Lynn McKinlay said it well:

    "We must take courage – we must know beyond a doubt that through the divine justice of the Lord, and because of His infinite foreknowledge, we were called and prepared and selected, because of our particular qualifications and capabilities, to come into the world in this generation ... and to do our specific work of being a light unto the Gentiles, and a savior to Israel ... in preparation for the coming of the Lord."

"So, we must continue with renewed determination in our labors of adapting and subjecting the elements of the flesh to the will of the Spirit, through obedience to all the ordinances of the Gospel that we have received, by obtaining forgiveness through complete repentance, ... and by using every gift and power and key of the knowledge of God that can be bestowed upon us in this world ..."[30]

What's more, as I have mentioned in previous letters, it is important for you to know with certainty that you are where you are now for reasons known to God. He has called you to your specific field of labor, from among the 340 missions the Church has around the world, to work with specific people that you are best suited to reach, to touch, and to teach. Our Father has children who reside in your area, whom He loves just as much as He loves you, whom He specifically needs you to find and introduce (or bring back) to the Gospel of Jesus Christ.

Let me cite an impressive example of this. I used to have a business partner named Mark (name changed). Mark has a large family and is a faithful member of the Church. He has a Scandinavian heritage that his parents and grandparents have kept alive in the family over the generations. As a young man, when he submitted his application to the Church to serve a mission, he and his family felt very strongly that he should be called to serve in a Scandinavian country given their proud ancestral tradition. In fact, they were so obsessed about it that Mark considered turning down the call if it were to a location other than his ancestral homeland. Needless to say, he and his family were absolutely elated when the call came for him to serve in Scandinavia.

During his time in the Language Training Mission (as it was called in those days), he had a difficult time learning the language. During his early months in the mission field, he continued to struggle with the language and with learning the missionary lessons. And that was not all. Unfortunately, he did not get along well with his companion. And finally, he became very sick. In fact, he was so ill that he needed medical care for several months in order to recover. Subsequently, it was necessary for him to return to the United States for a period of hospitalization and then home to convalesce.

Notwithstanding the difficulties he had experienced in the mission field, he was desirous of getting well so he might return to his mission in Scandinavia. At the time, he was not at all sure if it would actually happen.

One night he had a vivid dream. In the dream he was a healthy missionary again. He and his companion, who was unknown to him, were in the living room of a home teaching a lesson to a family. Upon waking, he distinctly remembered many details from the dream including the family members and where they sat in the room. He even remembered the furniture and other specifics about how the room was decorated. Mark believed this to be a sign that he would regain his health and return to Scandinavia to complete his mission.

When he was finally restored to good health, the Church did not send him back to Scandinavia. Instead he was sent to Alabama. Although somewhat disappointed, he humbly accepted the new assignment.

Upon meeting his new companion, Mark thought he looked familiar although they had not previously met. His companion said they needed to get going right away because they had a teaching appointment. They arrived at the home, sat down, and his companion began teaching. Since Mark wouldn't be doing the teaching, he had ample time to look around, examine the family, the room, and his companion. Then it hit him like a ton of bricks, he had seen all of this before. His companion, the family, and the room were all exactly as he had seen them in the dream he had when he was ill. Only then did he realize that *this* is where he was supposed to serve his mission, not Scandinavia.

Elder [ ], we should never try to dictate to the Lord, but we should always be accepting of His direction for us. Only He knows "the end from the beginning" and what our role is in His great work. Yes, it's all true!

As always, I remain.......
Your brother in the gospel,

Brother Dewey

Excerpts from Missionary Return Letters

Dear Bro. and Sis. Dewey
 Thanks so much for your letters. Things are going great here. We are teaching a lot of neat people.
 Yeah, the work keeps going well; we are bit by a dog or the rain's dumping on you, [but] the work never ceases.
 I love serving here and we are working really hard. So, yeah, I mostly wanted to say thank you for all you do and the wonderful people you are. I love you and keep the faith. And to echo you Bro. Dewey, it is for sure "all true"
Elder [ ]

Dear Bro. Dewey,
 I always love receiving your letters and they always have exactly what I need to hear in each one of them.
 I've been thinking of your friend Mark in relation to my missionary work. I realize how important it is to be the Lord's tool not guidance counselor. So thank you, you have given me great advice and something I can apply to my work to be more effective.
 The work is going well here. We are working hard and the Lord is blessing us with people to teach. The work is not easy but it's worth it and necessary.
 Thank you for all you do. I testify that it's true. Keep the faith.
 Your brother in the gospel and in the arms of the army of the Lord,
Elder [ ]

Letter Ten

Priesthood Authority

Dear Elder [ ],

    I trust this letter finds you well and still residing at the above address. I'm sure you had a great time talking to your family on Mother's Day. I hope you know how much Bonnie and I care for you. We take joy in your service and the growth you are experiencing in the growth process even though it's sometimes hard. One of the things I have learned in studying how to be a better disciple is that when we choose to follow Christ, we have to be "all in." We can't be only half way in because the Lord can't take only half of us to the celestial kingdom with Him.

    Several weeks ago, I tried to find my priesthood line of authority. Since we trace our individual lines of authority through our most recent priesthood ordination, I trace my authority from my ordination to the office of High Priest which occurred nearly 30 years ago under the hands of Elder Royden G. Derrick, of the Quorum of the Seventy, who was my former mission president. But try as I might, I couldn't find it in any of the logical places I looked. Although Elder Derrick passed away a couple of years ago, Sister Derrick is in quite good health for being in her 90's so I wrote her a letter asking if she might be able to provide it to me. A few days later I received a call from one of her sons, Jim, who read it to me over the phone. It went like this:

> DAVID S. DEWEY was ordained a High Priest by Royden G. Derrick on February 16, 1983.

ROYDEN G. DERRICK was ordained a High Priest by Harold B. Lee on October 15, 1948.

HAROLD B. LEE was ordained an Apostle by Heber J. Grant on April 10, 1941.

HEBER J. GRANT was ordained an Apostle by George Q. Cannon on October 16, 1881.

GEORGE Q. CANNON was ordained an Apostle by Brigham Young on August 26, 1860.

BRIGHAM YOUNG was ordained an Apostle on February 14, 1835, under the hands of the Three Witnesses: Oliver Cowdery, David Whitmer, and Martin Harris.

THE THREE WITNESSES were called by revelation to choose the Twelve Apostles and on February 14, 1835, were "blessed by the laying on of hands of the Presidency," Joseph Smith Jr., Sidney Rigdon, and Fredrick G. Williams to choose and ordain the Twelve Apostles.

JOSEPH SMITH JR. and OLIVER COWDERY were ordained to the Melchizedek Priesthood in 1829 by Peter, James, and John.

PETER, JAMES, and JOHN were ordained by the Lord JESUS CHRIST during His earthly ministry.

As Jim slowly read this vital information over the phone while I wrote it down, he did so with a great sense of respect and sacredness. As he spoke the names of the prophet Joseph Smith, of Peter, James and John, and the Lord Jesus Christ, I got goose bumps. The awesomeness of how we have a documented direct line of authority in the priesthood going back to Christ solemnly impacted me as never before. We are so blessed to have this privileged power and authority with us to bless the lives of others.

Early on in my mission, I had an experience that taught me much about the power of the priesthood. My companion and I had arrived early Sunday morning at the little LDS branch in Gateshead, England, for Church services. Within minutes the Branch President came looking for us. He said he had just received a call from the non-member husband of one of our member sisters who had been taken to the hospital. She had requested a priesthood blessing from the missionary elders. The branch president arranged for one of the members who had a car to take us to the hospital.

The only thing we knew was that the sister was having some kind of problem with her pregnancy. Upon our arrival at the hospital, we learned that she had a serious condition such that the doctor needed to deliver the baby, even though it would be precariously premature, or the mother's life would be in jeopardy. Either way, the life of the baby or the mother was at serious risk.

She asked me to be the voice for the blessing. Having just turned nineteen years old only a few months earlier, I had very limited experience with giving priesthood blessings and had never been involved in a blessing that was a matter of life and death for the recipient. Needless to say I was terrified inside. I tried to rely on the spirit and somehow managed to perform the blessing for this faithful sister. I don't recall now specifically what I said. Shortly thereafter I was transferred out of the area so I didn't hear how things turned out for her and her baby.

A couple of months later, I ran into my former companion at a missionary conference. I asked what happened with the sister. He said, "Oh, didn't you hear? She's doing just fine and she surprisingly gave birth to healthy *twins.*"

Closer to home, several months ago our ward bishop and stake president kindly paid us a visit at our home. Before leaving, they gave priesthood blessings to Bonnie and me. Within a few short days, I was experiencing noticeable improvement in my upper body where there had previously been none.

Elder [ ], I testify that the power of the priesthood is real. I have had too many experiences with it during my life to ever deny that knowledge. We typically don't share these miraculous stories with people generally because they are sacred to us who are believers. And even among us, we would never want to appear as boasting. We are indeed blessed that the Lord has been willing to share His power and authority with us to bless our fellow brothers and sisters if we live righteous, worthy and faithful lives. This is another great evidence to me that it's all true!

As always, I remain........

Your brother in the gospel,

Brother Dewey

Excerpts from Missionary Return Letters

Dear Brother Dewey,

I hope you know how much I love and appreciate your letters. In your last letter you spoke about the priesthood. My companion and I have spent the last transfer trying to figure out how we help these well meaning [people] understand how important the priesthood is without getting them offended. There are a lot of good churches out there that help people the best they can but will never get them the salvation they deserve [without the true authority of God].

I am so grateful for this time I have to serve my loving Heavenly Father. He has given me so many wonderful blessings. I've always been blessed with wonderful examples of priesthood leaders! I'm glad to count you as one of them!

I'm glad that you are seeing improvement in your health. Hope all is well.
Sister [ ]

Letter Eleven

Is Your Heart Right?

Dear Elder [ ],

Your parents were not able to make a contribution about you in the ward newsletter this month, so I don't know anything more about where you are or how you're doing since your last letter. No worries, however, because I know you serving faithfully and enjoying your mission.

In the July 2012 issue of the *Ensign* magazine, there was a short article on the last page entitled *Unspotted From The World* by Julie Thompson.[31] I hope you saw it. If not, I have enclosed a copy for your reference (see Appendix B). I can scarcely describe how impressed I was with this article.

In fact, I appreciated it so much that I did something I don't believe I have ever done before. I sent a comment to the editors of the magazine expressing my appreciation as follows:

"In the article in the July 2012 issue of the Ensign magazine entitled *Unspotted from the World*, Sister Julie Thompson offered a candid story about a Church service experience she had at the temple driven primarily by duty rather than love. When considered honestly, many of us may have similar feelings about our own service. Her remarkable transformation (change of heart) from a reluctant servant (self centered) to a true disciple (Christ centered) was a pointed lesson causing me deep introspection. Thank you for sharing this poignant experience and critically important reminder about how we should conduct our lives with true charity."

Although the sister in this article was doing good by volunteering to perform church service at a late night temple cleaning activity, she was, perhaps, doing it for the wrong reason. She candidly admitted that her attitude was not right. The scriptures say that such service is its own reward, because it's self-serving.

One may ask, as did author C. Terry Warner, "Do I love what I am doing, or do I love myself in doing it?" You see "self-righteousness ... is doing what's outwardly the right thing, but resentfully and grudgingly – and therefore proudly."[32]

Fortunately, a simple comment by a humble custodian got her spiritual attention resulting in her experiencing a "change of heart" about her task of cleaning the temple that night. More importantly, she reflected on all of her service, what she was doing and not doing in her life, and why. She came to realize that while she was living gospel principles and fulfilling assignments, perhaps, she was doing so to be "seen of men."

"As long as our hearts are wrong, we can't do right," said Brother Warner. Sister Thompson came to understand that she had been neglecting other things in her personal life and family life, and generally lacked true charity toward others. "Not *doing* right when we *know* what's right is doing wrong." Or, in other words, engaging in sins of omission. "How we respond to others requires something more than consideration and respect. It requires us not to just *act* honorably or kindly, but to *be* honorable and kind." Because "*who we are* is *how* we are in relation to others." Therefore, "when our hearts are right ... we feel to treat others generously [which] comes to us as an opportunity."[33]

I applaud this sister for writing such a beautiful article about her life changing experience and being courageous enough to submit it to the *Ensign* to have it published for all to read and learn from. Why? Because I can see myself in her mirror. If I am completely honest with myself, I, too, have to realize that I have been a fraud. This has also been made known to me through my study over this past year regarding true discipleship. I have a long way to go from being self-centered to being Christ-centered. I am working on it daily.

"The person I could be is very, very different from the person I am now, and becoming that person is worth any sacrifice," added Brother Warner.[34]

Sometimes the hardest part of the process is coming to understand the reality and life saving importance of these celestial principles and then humbly acknowledging the shortcomings that are preventing us from achieving our celestial goal. And then having the courage and internal strength of character to sincerely change our behavior and love others. We come to learn that we desperately need to kneel before the Lord and rely on the healing blessing of His atoning sacrifice and strive to have the Spirit to be with us to assist us in the process of change. And in this we find true joy and happiness.

Elder [ ], I have one last truism from Brother Warner, "We are infinitely worthwhile. Our measureless worth, which for me means our inherent goodness – has something to do with our capacity to respect and revere others."[35] I believe that you fall squarely in that category as demonstrated every day by your goodness and service to others. Thank you for being who you are and making the world a better place. God bless you this day and always.

As always, I remain.......

Your brother in the gospel,

Brother Dewey

Excerpts from Missionary Return Letters

Dear Brother Dewey,

Thank you so much for the letter! I love the article you sent from the Ensign. I ask myself all the time, "Am I doing this because it makes me look good? Or am I doing it because I love Heavenly Father?" That can be a hard switch to make if it isn't already your guiding force.

We are doing a Book of Mormon study that you might want to do with us. We are, as a mission, trying to read it before Christmas. As we read we are highlighting the doctrine of Christ in one color and His attributes in another. So if you want to do it you would need a clean copy.

Thank you for all your love and support!
Love,
Sister [ ]

Dear Brother Dewey,

Thank you so much for writing me! I love hearing from people back home. I really enjoyed your stories. I can't tell you how much it means to me to have uplifting letters to help me through the week.

How are you doing? I can't image how hard it must be to be homebound. I only know that things happen for a reason.

Personally my favorite part of serving a mission though, is how often Heavenly Father testifies to me how much He loves me. It always comes just when I need it most. It doesn't matter how many bad days or weeks we have when things like that happen they all disappear.

One of my first weeks here we didn't know where to go. We just drove and drove until finally we decided we were going to turn down the next street on the right. The next street was a dinky gravel road but we went down it anyway. There were only 3 or 4 houses on the street but we knocked anyway.

The third house we knocked at we met a nice woman who told us all about her trials and hard times. We prayed with her and she was shaking she was crying so hard. She really didn't want to know about the Church but we knew we had done what Heavenly Father wanted us to. He is so mindful of each and every one of us and he really does love us.

I hope all is well.
Sister [ ]

Letter Twelve

State of Becoming

Dear Elder [ ],

Your parents have been good to keep the ward informed about how you have been doing on your mission. I have really been pleased with that because I have very much appreciated hearing about you and some of your experiences. If I understand correctly, this will be my last correspondence before you return home. I thank you for putting up with my letters, sermons and personal stories. I'm sure they have done little for you, but I can't tell you how much it has meant to me, especially during my long period of convalescence. And thank you for your service. You will come to learn that your mission will have been one of the most important things you will have ever done in your life, for a variety of reasons.

I am pleased to report that my health has improved to the point that I have begun attending sacrament meetings again when I feel well enough. The first time back, Bonnie and I, with my walker, slipped into the back of the overflow seating in the cultural hall and sat down on the last row so as to not make a scene. Even though the bishopric had already taken their seats on the stand, they all walked back to greet us. After sacrament meeting, a number of other members were very kind to express their joy at having me back. My high priest group leader was so happy he had tears in his eyes and could hardly speak. I love them all so much. What a treat it was to be worshipping again among such good people!

Over the months, I have made several references in my letters about my quest to gain a better understanding of what it means to be a true disciple in Jesus Christ and how to better practice it. One thing I have learned with certainty is that it is a lifelong exercise. In fact, it is much more than an exercise, it is a life style developed day by day, moment by moment. Elder Neal A. Maxwell taught this when he said, "And so in this process of discipleship, we soon learn it is an incremental process. There has to be attention to the seemingly ordinary things as well as the seemingly ordinary people. I conclude that there are no ordinary people but there are likewise no ordinary moments. Also, this is part of coming to comprehend what discipleship is all about. Sobering, therefore, is the only word I can use regarding the dimensions of daily discipleship."[36]

There is much to contemplate in those words. One of the great concepts associated with true discipleship is that of loving others and losing yourself in their service. The reason Elder Maxwell said there are no "ordinary people" is because every person is of a divine nature and has the potential, through the atonement of Jesus Christ, to fulfill our Heavenly Father's plan for us to return to our heavenly home with Him and to activate the latent power within us to become Gods in the eternities. What a beautiful way to think of people in the here and now. It makes us more inclined to treat them in the way that God thinks of them, not so much for what they are today, but for what they are capable of *becoming*. This concept should be central to your missionary work.

Unfortunately, most of us seem to struggle with self-centeredness. This is part of the *natural man* in all of us.[37] It discourages us from rendering selfless service to our fellow beings. Brother C. Terry Warner, who I referred to in my last letter, states a grand principle: "Self-absorption (or self-centeredness) diminishes our capacity to give ourselves ... to other people, to our work, to play, to God, and to the beauty of nature."[38]

We must always be mindful, aware, and attuned to the needs of others.

And notwithstanding our good works, which are commendable and important, attaining the celestial kingdom and returning to the presence of the Father and the Son is possible only if those works are performed for the right reason; because we have experienced that *mighty change of heart* and have become new beings.[39] It's not just about what we have *done*; it's more about who we *are*.

Elder Dallin H. Oaks has taught, "The Final Judgment is not just an evaluation of a sum total of good and evil acts – what we have done. It is an acknowledgement of the final effect of our acts and thoughts – what we have become.

"This is achieved not just by doing what is right, but by doing it for the right reasons – for the pure love of Christ. The 'pure love of Christ' (Moroni 7:47) is not an act but a condition or state of being."[40]

Brother Robert L. Millet wrote, "Righteousness and pure religion are not just about doing things, even a lot of good things.

"In our heart of hearts we really do realize that what matters is the heart. In other words, while what we do certainly matters to God – we are called to be obedient disciples, to take up our cross daily, to deny ourselves of ungodliness, to follow him (Luke 9:23) – the real issue is, what are we *becoming*?

"One imposing challenge we face in this enlightened age is to get the gospel from our minds to our hearts, to seek for and allow the power of the blood of Christ to transform us into men and women who *do* what they say and, more important, also *are* what they *say*."[41]

Sadly, last month I lost a good friend who happily epitomized what I've just talked about. Dan's departure from this life came too early, he being just a few years older than me. I couldn't attend the funeral because of my health, so I wrote a letter to his good wife expressing how I felt about her husband in which I said, "I came to know what a fine man he was. His moral character and integrity were impeccable. He was honest to the core. He sincerely treated everyone with respect and love. He had an unwavering testimony of the gospel and strived to live it. What was said of Christ in 1 John 4:19 may be said of Dan, 'We loved him, because he first loved us.'"

You may want to consider this new motto that I am trying to adopt for myself: "Always do what's right, do it for the right reason, and do it right now."

May God bless you as you work to become the best missionary you can be and as you strive to become the best person you can be throughout your life.

Inspiration and Healing

We'll see you soon. As always, I remain.......
Your brother in the gospel,

Brother Dewey

Excerpts from Missionary Return Letters

Dear Brother Dewey and Bonnie,

It was good to hear from the both of you. I have to tell you that both of your letters were very needed this week. My self-worth has been under attack lately and knowing there are people at home, outside my family, that care and love me has been a great comfort. Of course, I consider both of you as part of my family and I thank Heavenly Father for putting so many wonderful people in my life.

I have learned so much about the gospel and people. People's motives and ideas can seem so weird sometimes. I think that's why we humans have a tendency to judge others. We usually don't understand where other people are coming from and so when their thought process is different than our own too many times we think it's wrong. Pride is a dangerous thing.

I have so many questions I want to ask Heavenly Father when I see Him but I wonder if any of them will matter anymore. I guess it's true what they say, "Everything I <u>need</u> to know I learned in Primary." Grownups make this too complicated.

I hope you don't mind I used part of one of your letters in a training meeting with some other missionaries. Your letters have helped me so much it just doesn't seem right to keep them to myself.

I can't wait to hear from you next month and see how you are doing. I love you both so much! Thank you for being great examples to me and our ward.

Love,
Sister [ ]

Letter Thirteen

Have Fun

Dear Sister [ ],

We really enjoyed receiving the photograph you sent of your smiling face. It brightened our day. And as far as any contribution Bonnie and I might have made to you and your mission, I think you have given us too much credit. We just enjoy being supportive of you. Also, I'm pleased to report that I have accepted your invitation to read the Book of Mormon every day along with you, marking as I go. It's always a beautiful experience.

It was wonderful for us to learn that you have been selected by your mission president to be a trainer. This clearly demonstrates how much confidence he and the Lord have in you. I know the Lord will bless you in this new responsibility. Yes, it is a challenge, but giving a new sister the right start will impact her for good throughout the rest of her mission. There's no question that you will be a great trainer.

You may have heard that Elder [ ] returned home and gave his homecoming address in sacrament meeting last week on the same day that [ ] gave his farewell address. I'm sure your parents and others will have communicated to you anything else that is noteworthy from home.

I think that my letters in recent months might have become a bit too intense and serious. So in this letter I've decided to tell a few short missionary and Church service stories from my experience that are on the lighter side. I'm sure you will have a few of your own fun stories to tell us about when you get home.

On my mission, I had a companion from Oregon who was a great guy and we had a lot of fun together – perhaps too much fun.

We were only together for six weeks, which was probably a good thing. One day we were knocking on doors and it was his turn to give the door approach. Usually we would stand closer together on the door step, but in this instance I stood back. As soon as the lady opened the door, I excitedly pointed to the ground at his feet and exclaimed, "A snake!" He was terrified of snakes. He yelped and jumped back looking down for the reptile all the while dancing his feet up and down like he was walking on hot coals. Then he realized I had "gotten" him. I had to repent and we didn't use that door approach again.

On another occasion, I was with my senior companion from Salt Lake City who wanted to tract in a well-to-do area. I told him I thought it may prove to be a waste of time to search out that area because, as Jacob said, "…wo unto the rich …for their hearts are upon their treasures; wherefore, their treasure is their god." (2 Nephi 9:30) But he wanted to work the area anyway. There were very few people home that day and those who answered their doors quickly and smugly dispensed with us like pests. One gentleman said he believed that it didn't much matter which church we belonged to because "all ships sail to heaven." Unfortunately, by that time my less than positive attitude had gotten the best of me and I responded with, "but you're on the Titanic." Again, I had to repent for being judgmental, for my lack of courteousness and had to make an attitude adjustment.

We had an elder in my mission who crashed not one but two mission cars. At least he was honest in explaining the cause of both accidents. His eyes had been distracted by girls wearing short skirts walking on the sidewalk. Needless-to-say he spent the rest of his mission on the bus or on his bike.

Years later, after Bonnie and I were married, I was called to be the first counselor in our ward bishopric. I believe I was 30 years old at the time and the bishop was only 28 years old. Just youngsters, imagine that! On one particular Sunday, sacrament meeting was just about to begin with the bishop conducting. He was seconds away from stepping up to the podium to begin the meeting when he suddenly handed me his agenda folder and anxiously said he had to leave for awhile, like he had some kind of emergency. I asked what the matter was. He said he just noticed that he had forgotten to shave that morning and needed to go home immediately. He quickly left out the side door of the chapel. I stood and told the congregation that the bishop asked to be excused but would rejoin us shortly.

On another Sunday, the second counselor in the bishopric was conducting the sacrament meeting. During much of the meeting he had his legs crossed, as was his custom. When it came time for him to stand to conclude the meeting, he uncrossed his legs, stood up, took one step toward the pulpit, and promptly fell to the floor. Apparently one of his legs had "gone to sleep" and was wobbly with no feeling. He pulled himself up by the podium and announced the conclusion of the meeting as if nothing had happened.

Perhaps there's room for just one more quick story with a visual aid. While serving in that same bishopric, we were holding ward council in the bishop's office early one cold winter's morning. The room was packed. We had just begun the meeting when the door opened and the young women's president rushed in asking to be excused for her tardiness. Since she saw no empty chairs, she walked toward the heating/air conditioning unit that protruded into the room below the window where some of the youth liked to sit during bishop's youth council. I suggested that it would be unwise for her to sit on the heating grate because she might get hot cross buns.

Believe it or not, "it's all true." (Maybe you had to be there.) I hope you are enjoying your mission and having some fun, but not so

much at the expense of others.
   As always, I remain.......
   Your brother in the gospel,

Brother Dewey

Excerpts from Missionary Return Letters

Dear Brother Dewey and Bonnie,

I really enjoyed your letter. Once again it came exactly when I needed it. We have the restored gospel, we should be the happiest people on earth, yet we often forget to have a little fun and laugh once in a while.

I loved the story about the companion you were with for only six weeks. It reminded me of my favorite companion. We were only together for five weeks but they were probably my happiest. I never felt judged but we could still talk about things we could improve on.

Thank you so much for your love and support.
Sister [ ]

Dear Dewey Family

Thank you so much for all the support you have given me the past few months. You will be happy to know I'm the happiest I think I have ever been in my life!

I am having so much fun with my new companion and we are growing closer to our Savior and Heavenly Father together. I LOVE being a missionary!
   MERRY CHRISTMAS!
Sister [ ]

Letter Fourteen

Pray Constantly

Dear Sister [ ],

    We particularly enjoyed your most recent letter and birthday greeting. Thanks, it was very thoughtful of you. I was especially pleased to learn that you are enjoying your new (green) companion. I chuckled out loud when you said, "She doesn't see the beauty in silence like I do."

    In my patriarchal blessing received a couple of weeks before leaving on my mission, it says, "Pray unto Him constantly in thy life that thou might be led and guided through the power of the Holy Ghost that He may touch thy mind and reveal unto thee the truths and principles of the gospel." Prayer has, in fact, been a constant source of help, comfort, truth and revelation for me throughout my life. I consider it to be one of the greatest blessings the Lord has given to me. May I share a few personal experiences with you regarding prayer?

    When I was a child, I lost something that was important to me at the time. In spite of searching "everywhere," I couldn't find the item, which was upsetting to me. As mentioned in a previous letter, I was fortunate to have had a mother who taught me at an early age to pray so I prayed to Heavenly Father to help me find the item. After offering a simple, believing, trusting, child's prayer, I promptly walked out into the back yard of our home and found the item in the grass beneath a tree. This is my earliest recollection of God answering my personal prayer.

    Early in our marriage, Bonnie and I lived in a duplex in the Holladay area of Salt Lake County. On the other side of the duplex lived an elderly widow. Her son, who was in the real estate business, owned the building. He was very particular about who he rented the apartment to because he wanted the tenants to be good neighbors to his aged mother. After we moved in and got acquainted with Mrs. Christensen, we grew quite fond of her and were happy to do anything we could to help her.

One summer's evening, it was approaching bed time when I realized I had forgotten to take the trash containers out to the street for collection the next morning. So I took our container out and then walked around to the back of Sister Christensen's apartment to retrieve the container that she kept just outside of her back door.

It was then that I heard a voice in the dark. Surprised and concerned I stood motionless trying to peer into the darkness. Since I saw and heard no one I continued on with my task. Then I heard the voice again. It seemed to be coming from her open bedroom window which alarmed me for fear there might be an intruder in her apartment. I quietly moved closer to the window. I then realized the voice I heard was Sister Christensen in the act of prayer. I knew this was a private moment for her and I had no business listening in, but I was somehow drawn to it because I had never heard anyone pray like her. She prayed as though her Heavenly Father was right there in the room with her. She really "knew" Him. This was a sacred place and I shouldn't be there so I quickly left. I will never forget what *that* kind of closeness to God sounds like and what it feels like. She gave me something to strive for in my personal prayers ever since.

Sister Wendy Ulrich expressed my feelings very well when she wrote, "I notice I am generally quite content to imagine God high in the heavens, listening from some far away throne room in my very human prayers. If I try to imagine instead inviting God to come close, to enter my little room and be seated nearby, I can hardly tolerate the emotions inherent in the image. I stop him at the perimeter, and even then I am flooded with fears and tears."[42]

Many years ago, I was engaged in a serious study of a certain gospel subject which was of great interest to me. After a year or two, I felt like I had exhausted all of the scriptural information and Church literature I could find on the topic. In not finding the answers to my queries I felt unfulfilled. Having done all I felt like I could do, I now felt justified in asking God, the Omniscient Father, directly in prayer regarding the matter. As it says about prayer in *Preach My Gospel*, "We will be enlightened, or given new knowledge."[43] I was just simple enough to believe, as I did when I was a child, that God would answer my supplication. I approached Him every day for several weeks asking for the enlightenment and knowledge about which I sought. Yet I received no answer. I began to feel that perhaps He didn't think I was worthy of the higher knowledge requested or that it was not needful for me to have it at that time.

Then, quite suddenly, I began to have thoughts come to my mind as if they were being poured into my head with a funnel. For two days my mind was flooded with what I can only describe as "pure knowledge." I became so mentally and emotionally overwhelmed with it all that my mortal soul could not continue to endure it. I fell to my knees and thanked God for the great blessing he had bestowed upon me, yet I had to ask Him to turn it off. It instantly stopped. Have you ever heard the old adage: be careful what you wish for because you just may get it?

Needless-to-say, during my illness I have prayed daily about my current health situation. Early on, I prayed that God would help me to endure it well and to learn those things that He wanted me to learn from the experience. During the worst nights, I prayed two or three times that He would just help me get through the night. More recently, I have prayed that He would help me learn to become a better disciple of Christ and give me the strength to overcome my weaknesses. Throughout it all I have offered many prayers of thanksgiving for the many "tender mercies" He has bestowed upon Bonnie and me.

Please know I have also regularly prayed for you while you have been serving on your mission. I have asked the Lord to bless you with safety and protection, for you to enjoy success in your selfless labors (as He may define "success" for you), that you might be led to those persons whom He has prepared for you to touch, and that you might find joy and happiness in His service.

Until we meet again, as always, I remain, your brother in the gospel.

Brother Dewey

Excerpts from Missionary Return Letters

Dear Dewey Family,

Thank you so much for the letters.

We have had a lot of wonderful things happen in our area and a lot of changes in our Mission. All of this has really strengthened my testimony and helped me understand the big picture. I know God is in control and what He needs to happen will. Isn't that comforting?

I love you both so much and I am grateful for your wonderful examples.

Sister [ ]

Dear Bro. Dewey,

I have been wanting to write you because I have to thank you for the great advice you gave me! It seems every letter you write me has something that I need at that particular time.

I have been trying so hard to help others better their lives but it seems like Satan just undoes everything. One night I prayed because I was down and I realized that God is aware of me and my efforts. He loves us and Satan can't stop this work from progressing! The next day great things happened for us, it's great to know God listens!

I'm doing well, I love being on a mission! Thank you for always writing me and supporting me. I pray that you may continue to heal and progress. Tell your wife hi for me, I love you both very much.

Love,
Elder [ ]

Letter Fifteen

Working Toward Perfection

Dear Sister [ ],

Now that Elder [ ] has returned from his mission in Minnesota, you have become the "senior" missionary serving from our ward. The contents of your last letter confirm how strong you have become and how much faith you have. You're great! I trust the Lord will bless you as you continue to work hard in the final weeks of your mission, with an eye single to the glory of God.

Wasn't it a surprising and great announcement President Monson made in General Conference about decreasing the age that young people may serve missions? About two weeks later, it was reported in the *Church News* that missionary applications were up over 500 percent, with slightly more than half of them being young women. This is so thrilling!

Today I would like to have us consider the subject of perfection. Now that is a lofty goal! Yet the Savior requires it of all of us when He declared it to the people in the Old World: "Be ye therefore perfect, even as your Father which is in heaven is perfect" (Matthew 5:48) and to the people in the New World: "Therefore I would that ye should be perfect even as I, or your Father who is in heaven is perfect" (3 Nephi 12:48). Lest we become discouraged by this command, consider the following thoughts taken from a book I just finished reading by David J. Ridges about the "signs of the times" leading up to the second coming of Christ.

The scriptures clearly reveal that the people on the earth who are living at the time of the Second Coming who are not living at least a terrestrial lifestyle will be destroyed (burned). So Brother Ridges wrote a chapter for those of us who may be concerned about how we're doing in that regard. He entitled it: *How Good Do You Have To*

Be In Order To Have a Pleasant Second Coming? He said a second question that can be asked which will help lead us to the answer to the first is: *"In order to be in the presence of God, do you have to be perfect?"*[44]

We know of scriptural references that say no *unclean* thing may dwell in the presence of God. But *clean* is not the same thing as *perfect*. Perfection, to my knowledge, was only achieved by one person during mortality and that person was Jesus Christ. Perfection for the rest of us will come along in due time after we have done all we can do in mortality and then continuing on after we have passed through the veil into the next life.

Elder Dallin H. Oaks made this clear when he taught, "Another idea that is powerful to lift us from discouragement is that the work of the Church ... is an eternal work. Not all problems ... are fixed in mortality. The work of salvation goes on beyond the veil of death, and we should not be too apprehensive about [our] incompleteness within the limits of mortality."[45]

The prophet Joseph Smith said, "It will be a great while after you have passed through the veil before you will have learned [all the principles of exaltation]. It is not all comprehended in this world; it will be a great work to learn our salvation and exaltation even beyond the grave."[46]

So we know that achieving perfection is highly unlikely for us in this life, therefore perfection cannot be the standard to qualify us to be present to welcome Christ at His Second Coming. However, it *is* required that we be clean, or as the scriptures say "spotless", to be in the presence of the Lord. Nephi said, "I have charity for my people, and great faith in Christ that I shall meet many souls *spotless* at his judgment-seat."(2 Nephi 33:7). This standard *is* possible during mortality. You see, at the time of Christ's coming we will experience, of necessity, a partial judgment to differentiate between the celestial and terrestrial people on the one hand, and the telestial people and sons of perdition on the other. So in order to have a pleasant Second Coming, we must be clean, or spotless, to be judged worthy to meet the Lord and not be burned.

We should not be confused, then, between perfect and spotless – they are different standards. With the help of the Savior and His Atonement, we can reach a point in this life where we are made clean, or spotless, and may thus qualify to be in His presence.

In Alma we read: "I beseech of you that ye not procrastinate the day of your repentance until the end... behold, if we do not *improve* our time while in this life, then cometh the night of darkness wherein there can be no labor performed.

"And this I know," Amulek testified, "because the Lord hath said he dwelleth not in unholy temples, but in the hearts of the righteous doth he dwell; yea, and he has also said that the *righteous* shall sit down in his kingdom, to go no more out; but their garments should be *made white through the blood of the Lamb*."[47]

With that said, Brother Ridges then makes an important point, "The word 'improve' in verse 33 above becomes a key word. If we do not improve we are in trouble. On the other hand, if we do improve, sincerely, we enable the Savior to make us clean through His Atonement (verse 36). Being made clean, we are spotless. Being spotless, we are allowed to be in the presence of God, where, as Joseph Smith pointed out in the previous quote, we can continue to progress until we become perfect."[48]

"Elder Marvin J. Ashton, of the Quorum of the Twelve, taught that the emphasis in the gospel of Christ is on *direction and diligence, not necessarily on speed*. He taught the importance of continuing improvement. In a General Conference address, he said:

"'The *speed* with which we head along the straight and narrow path isn't as important as the *direction* in which we are traveling.'"[49]

If you are alive when Christ comes again (and you might very well be), I sincerely hope you have a pleasant Second Coming.

Until we meet again, as always, I remain, your brother in the gospel.

Brother Dewey

P.S. I am still reading my Book of Mormon with you and have

read more than 350 pages now.

Excerpts from Missionary Return Letters

Hello!

I just wanted to send a quick note to say thank you! Y'all have been such a wonderful support for me on my mission. There were a couple of months I would not have been able to get through if it hadn't been for your cards, letters and love. Thank you so much for all you do.

See you soon.
Sister [ ]

Dear Dewey Family,

I just wanted to send you a quick note to let you know how much I love and appreciate all that you do for me. All the letters and love you send my way help more than you'll ever know. I am truly grateful to be here serving my Heavenly Father and brothers and sisters.

Serving a mission isn't easy but I can feel my testimony grow every day. I'm so blessed to have this time to build a relationship with Heavenly Father that will help me my whole life.

I love the gospel so much and I will always be indebted to the great teachers I've had.

I was glad to hear your health is improving! Good health is something I think a lot of people take for granted. Hope all is well!

Love,
Sister [ ]

Letter Sixteen

The Standard of Truth Will Prevail

Dear Elder [ ],

Thank you for your card received here on Saturday. Once again you have been very thoughtful toward us. I'm sure you would have gotten through those difficult couple of months without us, but it was kind of you to say that we may have been of some long distance help.

Last month we spoke somewhat of preparing for the Second Coming of Christ. When we consider the condition of the world in the "last days" it can be easy for us to focus too much on the tribulations, wickedness, wars and natural calamities that are now and will yet envelope the earth. Notwithstanding, we must not despair or get discouraged; rather we should always remember that light and truth will triumph over darkness and evil. We know how this story ends.

In fact, regarding the last days, the Lord was including your missionary service when He said, "Righteousness and truth will I cause to sweep the earth as with a flood, to gather out mine elect from the four corners of the earth" (Moses 7:62). Brother Craig James Ostler in his new book *Refuge from the Storm* stated: "The iniquity of the last days is countered by the righteousness of God's kingdom. The good of all nations have refuge from the storm in the stakes of Zion. Like a great flood, the power of virtue and the strength of truth moves forward, gathering the righteous to the Church of Jesus Christ."[50]

Isn't it wonderful to be so intimately involved in the great work of the Lord in these latter-days; to stand as a witness for Him and His gospel to all nations and peoples? You have been called to be among the Lord's mightiest representatives, serving on the front lines in the great gathering of Israel in preparation for the Second Coming of Christ. And as such, the Lord has said, "You shall have my Spirit and my word, yea, the power of God unto the convincing of men" (D&C 90:9, 11). What a tremendous blessing, honor and privilege you have. I thrill at the very thought of it! Clearly, there is no need to despair.

Late last month, I took a trip down memory lane by recounting my own full-time missionary experience. I began by reading my missionary journal. You might recall I served in what was then called the England North Mission way, way back in the early 1970s. I still have letters from people I had the privilege of finding, teaching and baptizing who had corresponded with me for years afterward. In each instance, they expressed how blessed and grateful they felt because I had chosen to serve a mission and had found them and brought them out of obscurity and darkness into the beautiful light of the restored Gospel of Jesus Christ and His Church. Their lives were changed forever and I believe we will be wonderful friends throughout eternity. I came away from my little journey back in time so inspired and spiritually moved that I wondered how I might find a way to join you and serve as a full-time missionary again. You, too, have new friends who consider you in equally high regard. You will have blessed not only them, but their posterity for generations to come if they remain faithful. This is how long-lastingly beautiful your missionary experience will be for you and for those with whom you have served. It's all very humbling.

And the work will go on as the Prophet Joseph Smith so boldly declared, "The Standard of Truth has been erected; no unhallowed hand can stop the work from progressing; persecutions may rage, mobs may combine, armies may assemble, calumny may defame, but the truth of God will go forth boldly, nobly, and independent, till it has penetrated every continent, visited every clime, swept every country, and sounded in every ear, till the purposes of God shall be accomplished, and the Great Jehovah shall say the work is done."[51] This is so powerful! I get goose bumps every time I read it.

Elder [ ], you are engaged in the great work the prophet spoke of and I honor and respect you for serving so honorably. I know you have experienced much personal growth during your mission. You have learned skills, developed insights, and obtained knowledge and experience which will help you throughout your life. And more importantly, you have served God and His children with love and dignity.

Since this is my last letter to you, I want to thank you for putting up with me these past many months. Although I'm sure my letter writing has been unremarkable for you, the experience has brought me much joy and has been therapeutic during my long recovery. And you have been so kind and considerate to write back to us in cards and letters. Thank you very much. You are so sweet. May God continue to bless you all the days of your life.

As I have said before, it's all true! That's my simple, succinct, firm, and abiding testimony which sustains me through thick and thin. How I love the Gospel of Jesus Christ and His Church. Until we meet again (soon), I remain, your brother in the gospel.

Brother Dewey

Excerpts from Missionary Return Letters

Brother Dewey,
Thank you very much for sharing this wonderful advice with me. I am grateful that my dad has great friends like you. Thank you for always knowing just what I need to hear at the right time. I don't know everything, but I do know that we are all Heavenly Father's children and He knows just how to help us. I hope to be able to do what is said in the letter about giving [my] all and working hard. I hope to come home every night feeling tired physically as well as spiritually. Thanks for everything. I am really loving this experience out here. I have learned so much in such a short amount of time. I love learning and growing every day. I know that you are being a great

servant of the Lord. I can feel your love for Him and I am grateful for that. You have inspired me to do better every chance I get. Thanks. Much love from here.
Elder [ ]

Letter Seventeen

Working for the Living and the Dead

Dear Elder [ ],

In the ward newsletter your parents wrote about how things are going for you and it was quite informative. Many of us here at home are very proud of your faithful service. Keep up the good work.

Sadly, we have had three funerals in the ward over the last several weeks that have, in part, prompted me to write about this month's topic.

Many years ago I obtained a booklet containing a discourse by Elder Melvin J. Ballard, a former member of the Quorum of the Twelve Apostles, given in 1922. Recently I read a quote from that sermon which caused me to find the booklet and reread the entire discourse. Elder Ballard addressed a great concept regarding the work you have been doing on your mission and that you will yet do during your life and how they are connected.

Elder Ballard asked, "Why is it that sometimes only one of a city or household receives the Gospel? It was made known to me that it is because the righteous dead who had received the Gospel in the spirit world [are] exercising themselves, and in answer to their prayers elders of the Church were sent to the homes of their posterity that the Gospel might be taught to them and through their righteousness they might be privileged to have a descendant in the flesh do the work for their dead kindred. I want to say to you that it is with greater intensity that the hearts of the fathers and mothers in the spirit world are turned to their children than that our hearts are tuned to them."[52]

As you know, there is also an intensive missionary program going on in the spirit world for those who had no opportunity to receive the Gospel of Jesus Christ during their mortal lives. Wilford

Woodruff, fourth president of the Church, stated: "The same priesthood exists on the other side of the veil. Every man who is faithful is in his quorum there."[53] What's more, Joseph F. Smith taught, "...good sisters who have been set apart, ordained to the work...will be fully authorized and empowered to preach the gospel and minister to the women while the elders and prophets are preaching to the men."[54] He also taught, "The things we experience here are typical of the things of God and the life beyond us."[55]

Elder Neal A. Maxwell provided this insightful observation when he said: "On the other side of the veil, there are perhaps seventy billion people. They need the same gospel, and releases occur here to aid the Lord's work there. Each release of a righteous individual from this life is also a call to new labors."[56]

The family history work and genealogical research we do for our deceased ancestors, which results in baptisms and other ordinances performed in their behalf in our temples, is missionary work for those in the spirit world as our hearts are turned to our fathers. What we don't often consider is how much influence they may be having on the work here.

Elder Ballard told this remarkable story in his discourse: "I recall an incident in my own father's experience. How we looked forward to the completion of the Logan [Utah] temple! It was about to be dedicated. My father had labored on that house from its very beginning, and my earliest recollection was carrying his dinner each day as he brought the rock down from the quarry. I remember how in the meantime father made every effort to obtain all the data and information he could concerning his relatives. It was the theme of his prayer night and morning that the Lord would open the way whereby he could get information concerning the dead.

"The day before the dedication, while writing recommends to the members of his ward who were to be present at the first service, two elderly gentlemen walked down the streets of Logan, approached my two younger sisters, and, coming to the older one of the two, placed in her hands a newspaper and said: 'Take this to your father. Give it to no one else. Go quickly with it. Don't lose it.'

"The child responded and when she met her mother, her mother wanted the paper. The child said, 'No, I must give it to father and no one else.'

"She was admitted into the room and told her story. We looked in vain for these travelers. They were not to be seen. No one else saw them. Then we turned to the paper. The newspaper, *The Newbury Weekly News*, was printed in my father's old English home, Thursday, May 15, 1884, and reached our hands May 18, 1884, three days after its publication. We were astonished, for by no earthly means could it have reached us, so our curiosity increased as we examined it. Then we discovered one page devoted to the writings of a reporter of the paper, who had gone on his vacation, and among other places had visited an old cemetery. The curious inscriptions led him to write what he found on the tombstones, including the verses. He also added the names, dates of birth, death, etc., filling nearly an entire page.

"It was the old cemetery where the Ballard family had been buried for generations, and very many of my father's immediate relatives and other intimate friends were mentioned.

"When the matter was presented to President Merrill of the Logan Temple he said, 'You are authorized to do the work for those [people], because you received it through messengers of the Lord.'

"There is no doubt that the dead who had received the Gospel in the spirit world had put it into the head of that reporter to write these things, and thus the way was prepared for my father to obtain the information he sought, and so with you who are earnest in this work, the way shall be opened."[57]

Elder [ ], I testify to you that the great missionary work, whether for the living or for the dead, is all about the same goal – to assist Heavenly Father's children, our brothers and sisters, to return to His presence and experience again the exceptional love and great joy which can only be found in His light. To quote Brother Andrew C. Skinner, "Our vicarious efforts in the temple are the culmination of all the missionary labors in the spirit world, just as the temple is the desired culmination of our missionary labors here in mortality"[58]

Inspiration and Healing

As I have said many times before, it's all true! That's my simple, succinct, firm, and abiding testimony which sustains me through my afflictions. How I love the Gospel of Jesus Christ and His Church. Until we meet again (soon), I remain....

Your brother in the gospel,

Brother Dewey

Excerpts from Missionary Return Letters

Brother Dewey,
　　Thank you for the letter Brother Dewey, I always enjoy reading your monthly notes. I hope you are well.
Elder [ ]

Letter Eighteen

Modern Apostles and Prophets

Dear Elder [ ],

It was wonderful to hear about the baptism of your investigator, and a double-dipper, no less, since he was not completely immersed under the water the first time. The work of salvation continues one brother or sister at a time. Keep up the good work. May God continue to bless you in your selfless service.

We are so fortunate to have modern prophets and apostles among us in our time as it has been in previous times. A prophet is a man called of God by revelation to be His mouthpiece and His messenger on the earth. They were numbered among the premortal "noble and great ones."[59] They were foreordained for their specific missions. They can see things "afar off" (D&C 101:54), in order to envision the truth and to speak the truth. Prophets can also function as seers, revealing "secrets" or "hidden things "which are not known."[60] They declare repentance to the people and invite all to come unto Christ and be saved in Him.

Modern revelation designates apostles as "special witnesses of the name of Christ in all the world" (D&C 107:23). They work under the direction of the prophet and president of the Church.

These are truths we must come to know to be true; of which we must have a firm testimony.

I had a friend who returned home from his mission in California when I had been out on my mission for about six months. He told this story about how he gained a testimony of the modern Apostles and Prophets of the Lord.

On his way to the mission field and during the early weeks of his mission, he began to wonder what he was doing there among strangers. He wondered if the modern apostles are really apostles of

Inspiration and Healing

the Lord and was the President of the Church truly a prophet of God. So he earnestly prayed and asked Heavenly Father if He would reveal to him if they really were His true apostles and prophets.

A short time later, Elder Boyd K. Packer, a member of the Quorum of the Twelve Apostles, came to speak at the stake conference in his area. The day of the conference he was given the impression to fast, but he hesitated to respond to the prompting. When the impression came to him again he decided to obey and go to the conference in the manner of fasting.

At the Saturday evening session of the conference, the missionaries sat on the front row of the stake center. He felt impressed to look at the time on his watch. It was 6:30pm which reminded him that it was 5:30pm at his home in Utah, the exact time his family would be on their knees surrounding the kitchen table for their evening meal and praying for him.

Thirty minutes later when the conference was about to begin, he had another impression that he would bear his testimony in the meeting. He thought how absurd that notion was since he wasn't on the program and certainly he couldn't and wouldn't just walk up to the pulpit and bear his testimony without an invitation.

The meeting began as usual, but just before it was time for the scheduled speakers to begin, he noticed Elder Packer whisper something to the stake president. When the stake president stood up to the pulpit to speak, instead of beginning his prepared talk, he invited my friend to please come up to the stand and bear his testimony before the large congregation.

On his way up to the pulpit, Elder Packer stood and shook his hand. He said although Elder Packer didn't speak a word to him, as he looked into his eyes he plainly heard the words, "This is an apostle of the Lord, he is a servant of the living God, and Harold B. Lee is a prophet of God." His prayer had been answered in a remarkable way.

Many years ago, when our family lived in another stake in the Salt Lake Valley, Elder Richard G. Scott, of the Quorum of Twelve Apostles, was the visiting General Authority at stake conference. At the Saturday evening session, he announced that President Ezra Taft Benson, the president of the Church at that time, would make a surprise appearance at the conference session the next morning. Word spread quickly that we were to have the rare honor of having the prophet attend our local conference. On Sunday morning the chapel and overflow were filled to capacity with members who were excited to see and hear the prophet. I was seated on the front row, right side, of the chapel where the leaders would enter the chapel. As soon as the prophet and his wife walked into the chapel, right in front of me, the congregation stood out of respect and honor for him in his capacity as the Lord's anointed prophet. It was a joy for us to hear him speak and to receive a blessing from him.

Elder [ ], I have spoken several times in previous letters about some of my treasured personal experiences with modern prophets and apostles. I can testify of their divine missions and their greatness as representatives of the Lord Jesus Christ on the earth, having been foreordained to such in the premortal existence. There is safety and salvation in following the prophets and obeying their wise and prophetic counsel. I have a firm testimony of this truth. As I am fond of saying, "It's all true!"

Until we meet again, I remain....

Your brother in the gospel,

Brother Dewey

Excerpts from Missionary Return Letters

Dear Brother Dewey,

Wow. Really there is no way to thank you so much for all your letters. They inspire me to be a better missionary. I am grateful for your testimony. It inspires me.

I love the people here and they have a very soft spot in my heart. Being a missionary has changed me forever and I have come to know the goodness of the Lord and the importance of the scriptures. How blessed we are to have them. The very

words of Jesus Christ. I love Him and I love you, Brother Dewey.
Thank you for your dedication. You will always be a great example to me.
Much love,
Elder [ ]

Letter Nineteen

Miracles Accompany This Work

Dear Elder [ ],

In a recent stake conference in the Utah County area, the stake president described an experience he had as a young missionary in the Midwest which speaks to the beauty of missionary work and how both giver and receiver are blessed.

He and his companion walked up to the door of a home and knocked three times. No one answered so they knocked three more times. Still no answer, so they knocked three times again. They had turned to walk away when an older African-American lady opened the door. Because it had begun to rain, the women invited them into her home and told them her story. She had bad health, her husband had died, and she was left all alone. After 20 minutes of her doing all of the talking she asked them, "Do you have something to tell me?"

The elders told her who they were and proceeded to give her the first missionary discussion. Before they left they gave her a copy of the Book of Mormon and a sheet of paper with a list of recommended scriptures she could read from the book.

The elders didn't think much more about their visit and neither one felt as though anything would become of it so they didn't consider putting her on their follow-up list.

Three or four weeks later, however, they decided to stop by to see the old woman.

They arrived at her home and knocked on the door three times. She did not answer, so they knocked three more times. Still no answer, so they knocked three times again. Finally the lady opened the door and let them in to visit. Again, she told them her story for 20 minutes, repeating what she had told them on their first visit. When she was done, she asked them again, "Do you have something to tell me?"

They asked her if she had read any of the scriptures in the Book of Mormon from the sheet of paper they had left her from their last visit. She told them she read the Sermon on the Mount and how she understood it better from *their* scriptures than she had from the New Testament. She talked about the brothers Lamen and Lemuel; how everything was so hard for them. She talked about how they were so bad and yet they still had the desire to be with their family. And then, much to the surprise of the elders, she talked about the book of Doctrine and Covenants. They hadn't mentioned that book to her during the first visit.

With the help of the elders, she started to attend Church with them. Because of her poor health and general weakness associated with her advanced age, she was forced to use a cane while walking. The elders needed to assist her in and out of the Church building. A short time later she was baptized a member of the Church.

You may think this is the end of a good conversion story, but hold on. A short while later the elders went to visit the lady. They knocked on the door three times and the same thing happened as before. No one answered so they repeated this two more times until the sister answered.

She was very pleased to have the elders there. With much excitement she told them she had obtained her "life script" and she wanted them to read it to her. They didn't understand what she meant by her life script. When she handed the paper to them they realized she was talking about her patriarchal blessing that she had recently received from the stake patriarch. They were hesitant to read it explaining to her that it was a blessing from our Heavenly Father and it is a personal matter between her and Him. She continued trying to persuade them to read it to her and they continued to say why they thought it was inappropriate for them to read her personal blessing.

Then she said to them, "You don't know."

They replied, "Know what?"

She said, "The Lord opened up my *heart* so I would know and feel that the scriptures are true, but He also opened my *eyes* so that I could read the scriptures by myself. I have been blind for years."

The elders were shocked! Somehow they hadn't known. Humbled, they were honored to read the things the Lord had promised her in her patriarchal blessing.

The dear lady passed away very shortly thereafter.

Elder [ ], can there be any question that the Lord loves His children and has prepared some of them for you to find, teach, and baptize into His true Church. Miracles accompany this great work.

Until we meet again, I remain....

Your brother in the gospel,

Brother Dewey

Excerpts from Missionary Return Letters

Brother Dewey,
 Thanks for your letters. They mean a lot!
Elder [ ]

Letter Twenty

Sanctification

Dear Elder [ ],

I have often contemplated about what great value it is for a young man (or woman) to serve a full-time mission. I believe you have been out on your mission long enough that I can share what I have learned about this topic with you. May I begin by first citing a story from my own mission which will shed some light on this subject?

During the period while I was serving in the mission home (office), we had an elder in one of the districts who had been out for only a short time when he decided that a mission wasn't for him and he had decided to go home. This elder was from an Idaho farm family who had tilled the earth for generations. All he ever wanted to do was to get married to a sweet girl and be a farmer. He really loved and understood the land. He enjoyed lifting the soil with his hands and feeling it slip through his fingers. He was on the quiet and shy side, as I recall, rather uncomfortable with people, but otherwise a nice, pleasant young man.

He was brought into the mission home for a few days. The mission president talked with him at length on several occasions about all the reasons why he should stay and serve an honorable mission, but nothing changed his mind. He was determined to return home.

It just so happened at that very time a General Authority came to visit our mission. So the mission president arranged for him to meet with the determined missionary. I remember well how anxious we all were when just the two of them went into the mission president's office and closed the door behind them. It seemed like about an hour later when they came out. Imagine our surprise and delight when the elder emerged smiling and "fired up" about staying out on his mission. He was soon on the next train back to his assigned area. He went on to fulfill an honorable mission.

For years I wondered what had happened in that room that day to change his attitude. When he made an appearance at one of our mission reunions, I saw an opportunity to finally learn the answer. At an appropriate time I pulled him aside and asked him to tell me about it. He was pleased to relate the story.

He said the General Authority "worked him over pretty good" and basically talked about the same things the mission president had talked to him about. But he was not impressed to change his mind about going home. He said there came a point when the General Authority finally stopped talking, leaned back in his chair, and turned to gaze out of the window as if he was ready to give up on him. He thought the ordeal was over. Then he saw a change come over the General Authority's face, a kind of wry smile appeared on his lips. He leaned forward and in a calm voice but commanding spirit, he said that if he did not stay and serve an honorable mission, that he would marry the wrong girl and, what's more, his crops wouldn't grow. The young elder said he knew by the spirit that enveloped them at that moment that he was being told the truth and it was coming from God. He said he couldn't let those things happen so he had a change of heart and stayed in England to serve a faithful mission.

Elder William R. Bradford, an emeritus member of the Quorum of the Seventy, gave a very powerful talk in General Conference about those who should and could serve missions but who choose not to serve. He said:

"It causes me to wonder if they really understand and believe the twofold nature of the purpose of missionary work: first, to sanctify the missionary himself, and second, to bring converts to a knowledge of the truths of the restored gospel of Jesus Christ and to baptism into His Church—which is the sure and natural product of a missionary who is in the process of sanctification.

"If I could speak separately to each of you young men and your parents who so justify, I would say with all the power of speech I could generate, 'Just who do you think you are? What right do you have to match your wisdom with that of God, who through His prophets has issued a firm decree, a solemn mandate, that the restored gospel must be declared to all the world by the voice of His disciples? This means you!'

"I would say to you that you are left without excuse and without justification and that you have placed your eternal salvation in grave danger.

"This is a marvelous plan. It is a process of sanctification. When a missionary is placed in a mission environment of order and discipline where all that is done is in harmony with the Spirit, the missionary experiences a great transformation. The heavens open. Powers are showered out. Mysteries are revealed. Habits are improved. Sanctification begins. Through this process the missionary becomes a vessel of light that can shine forth the gospel of Jesus Christ in a world in darkness.

"Missions are for missionaries. It is a marvelous gift of time, a time given when you can experience glimpses of heavenly life here on earth. It is a time of cleansing and refreshing. It is a special time when the Holy Ghost can seal upon you the knowledge of the great plan for your exaltation. It is one of your best opportunities to become a celestial candidate.

"The teaching and conversion of others is the natural product of this process. To sanctify yourself you must serve others. The highest of all service to others is to teach them truth and bring them into the kingdom of God."[61]

Therein is encapsulated the value of serving an honorable mission.

Until we meet again, I remain....

Your brother in the gospel,

Brother Dewey

Inspiration and Healing

Excerpts from Missionary Return Letters

Brother Dewey,

    I wanted to write to thank you for all of your letters you have been sending me and especially the last one. I feel like I have changed quite a bit on my mission and I know that it is a great start for the rest of my life.

    I am thankful that The Lord gives us a new chance everyday to forsake our sins and to serve him with all diligence. I have a testimony that we have the Gospel to help make the change from being bad to good, [from] sinners to disciples of Jesus.

    I am glad that we all have the callings to be missionaries to help others as well.

Thanks for everything, Brother Dewey.

Elder [ ]

Letter Twenty-One

Angels Assist with This Work

Dear Elder [ ],

The more I learn about the gospel, the more I have come to learn of how the missionary work in mortality is assisted by those from the other side of the veil. Recently I read a book by Donald A. Parry, a professor at BYU. I was particularly impressed with this statement he made, "During the last days…angels are inviting people to repent. Angels are also assisting in gathering the elect from all nations. In this capacity, they are co-workers with our full- and part-time missionaries."[62] Isn't it wonderful and humbling to know that you and your investigators might have had the help of angels from the other side? I'm sure you can look back on some of the experiences you have had on your mission and you can see how this has been true. And you can't even imagine all of the other instances of heavenly assistance and protection that you don't even know about.

As you know, the great missionary work continues on the other side of the veil as the gospel of Jesus Christ is taught to those who did not have the opportunity of receiving it during their mortal lives on the earth. Those who have accepted it are waiting for us to perform the saving and exalting ordinances for them in the temples; temples which are increasing dotting the earth. We often hear of experiences of assistance from beyond the veil with regard to the great work which is going on for our deceased ancestors, with family history research, and within our temples.

A fellow high priest and his good wife have been fine neighbors and friends to us for many years. They have both served in the Jordan River Temple for a number of years. He has told me on several occasions of how there is hardly a week goes by that he doesn't have some type of spiritual experience in the temple. Recently he told me this story.

The last live endowment session of the day was within about ten minutes of finishing when he saw a couple standing in the foyer of the temple that looked confused or a bit lost. My friend approached the couple and asked if he might help them in some way. They explained they had come a considerable distance to participate in the endowment session of a relative. Unfortunately, they had been unavoidably detained causing them to arrived too late to attend the session. They asked if it would be possible for them to be permitted to greet their party in the celestial room following the session. My friend said he would be happy to assist them with their request.

However, the man didn't have a pair of white pants and his wife didn't have a white dress, but they had the other temple clothing they needed. My friend explained that since there were no more sessions that evening, the clothing rental counter was closed so there were no workers there to help them obtain the clothing they needed. One of the sister temple workers had come by in time to hear their situation and said to the visiting sister, "I'm just about your size, let me go to my locker and get you a dress I have there." With that lead, my friend provided a pair of his own temple pants for the brother to use. After the couple had changed into their temple clothing, they were escorted to the celestial room all the while expressing their gratitude for the kind assistance they had received.

Later that evening, as my friend was closing the temple for the night with one of his co-workers, he learned that his co-worker had been assisting the group in the session attended by the people my friend had assisted earlier. The co-worker said he had heard about the incident with the visitors and how he had provided a pair of his own pants for the brother. Then he asked, "By the way, how did you communicate with them?"

"What do you mean?" responded my friend. "I spoke to them and they spoke back, of course."

"You couldn't have," said the co-worker. "You don't speak Spanish and that couple didn't speak English."

The Lord doesn't much distinguish between this life and the next when it comes to the work of salvation. So when we live faithful lives and are worthily working in His service among His children, He will provide us with the help we need to accomplish the work by whatever means best suit His purposes which may, at times, seem like miracles to us. I know this is true. In fact, it's all true.

Until we meet again, I remain....

Your brother in the gospel,

Brother Dewey

Excerpts from Missionary Return Letters

Brother Dewey,

Thank you so much for all of the letters and encouragement that you have sent to me [during] this time. I have very much enjoyed reading them, and they have helped me more than you know.

Thank you for being my brother in the Gospel, and I'll be seeing you in just a bit.

May God bless you,
Elder [ ]

Letter Twenty-Two

What is a Missionary?

Dear Elder [ ],

When my mother was alive and living in a local health care center, I made regular visits to see her. On one such visit, I entered through the main doors of the building, signed in at the lobby desk, and made a right turn down the main hallway. There was no one besides me in the long corridor. As I walked along, an old woman in a wheelchair entered the hallway at the other end. She was slowly pushing herself along without looking up. I had always tried to be friendly to everyone I met there and had come to know some of the residents and recognized others, yet I couldn't identify this lady. Perhaps she was new to the facility.

As we drew close to one another, she stopped pushing her chair and raised her head to look up at me. I was pleased she had stopped so that I could greet her. I stopped walking, looked into her eyes and smiled, but still didn't recognize her. I thought her face expressed confusion. She didn't smile back but asked me a question with some concern in her voice, "How do I get there?"

"Well, now, that all depends on where you're going," I cleverly responded.

Then she said longingly, "I want to go to heaven."

She broke my heart. I was speechless and didn't know quite how to respond to her. She must have observed this by the expression on my face because her face then changed to a witty grin and she said, "But not right *now*."

I know that's what it's like as you approach the end of your mission. Of course you want to go home, but not right now. Why? Because you finally have it down; you have learned the language; you know how to teach the Gospel; and you have come to love the

Inspiration and Healing

people you have served. You know there is so much more work to be accomplished. You will miss so much; the people, the culture, the experiences, your fellow missionaries, the blessings, the spirit, the love, the growth, and much more.

Many years ago, while I was serving as a full time missionary, my mother sent me this message she found in an unidentified Church publication. It is entitled "What is a Missionary?" Although it is somewhat dated in some of its references, it is still an apt description of missionaries today.

> Somewhere between the whirl of teenage activity and the confinement to come of the rocking chair, we find a strange creature called a missionary.
>
> Missionaries come in assorted varieties of Elders and Lady Missionaries. They come in assorted sizes, weights, and colors – green being the most common among the new ones.
>
> Missionaries are found everywhere – hurrying to, climbing up, knocking on, walking through, preaching to, and getting thrown out of. Converts love them, young girls worship them, the law tolerates them, most people ignore them, and heaven protects them.
>
> A missionary is a composite. It has the appetite of a horse, the enthusiasm of a fire cracker, the patience of Job, the persistence of a Fuller Brush salesman, and the courage of a lion tamer.
>
> It likes letters from home, invitations to Sunday dinners, conferences, checks, and visits from the Mission President.
>
> It isn't much for blizzards, ladies who slam doors, hats, suits, dull ties, apartment houses, transfers to hot areas, shaking hands at arm's length with the opposite sex, alarm clocks, or letters that begin with "Dear John."
>
> A missionary is truth with a pocket full of tracts, wisdom with scant knowledge of the lessons, plus a good

serious companion; and faith with sixty-nine cents in its pocket.

Nobody else can knock so boldly with such a shaky hand. Nobody else can get such a thrill at the end of a discouraging day from the words, "Come right in, I've been waiting for you to call." Nobody else is so early to rise or so tired by 10:00 p.m.

Yes, a missionary is an odd character. It can get homesick, discouraged, and temporarily lose faith in the whole human race, but a strange lump will rise it its throat the day it receives its letter of release; and on arrival home its homecoming speech will probably contain the phrase it once considered trite, "The time I spent in the 'mission field' was the happiest time of my life."

Elder [ ], since this is my last letter to you, I want to thank you for putting up with me these past many months. Although I'm sure my letter writing has been unremarkable for you, the experience has brought me much joy and has been therapeutic toward my lengthy healing and recovery. And you have been so kind and thoughtful to write back on several occasions. Thank you so much. May God continue to bless you all the days of your life as you boldly take hold of your future.

As I have said many times before, it's all true! This simple, succinct, firm, and abiding testimony has sustained me through thick and thin. I love the Lord. I love the restored Gospel of Jesus Christ and His Church. Until we meet again (soon), I remain....

Your brother in the gospel,

Brother Dewey

Excerpts from Missionary Return Letters

Brother Dewey,
Thank you so much for your letters. They are very inspiring

to me. How are you doing? How is your health? I have been praying for you.

Things here are amazing. I love being a missionary. It is something that I have really grown to love. The people here are amazing. I know that this is the only place the Lord wants me to be right now. We are teaching a lot of people that I have grown to love very much. I hope everything goes well for you Bro. Dewey.

Sincerely,

Elder [ ]

Dear Brother Dewey,

My parents told me you got my letter, great! I hope you enjoyed it as much as I enjoy your letters.

Thankfully we have a loving Heavenly Father who desires us to be like him. Sometimes we have trials in our lives that help us grow. Though your illness has been a trial for you, I have no doubt that you have grown immensely in your patience and overall spirituality. Or as Job said, "When he hath tried me, I shall come forth as gold." Never forget, Brother Dewey, that you shall "come forth as gold" after your trial.

I know the Lord loves each and every one of us. I hope that we can continue to grow every day in our lives so we can be perfected through him whom we love.

I remain your brother in the faith,

Elder [ ]

Afterword

Dear Reader,

People who have known me throughout my health ordeal will now say to me, "You look good." It's difficult to know exactly what they really mean, but if they mean I have gained my weight back and, therefore, my face isn't as gaunt and drawn as it was during the worst period of my illness, or that I am no longer using a walker or two walking sticks to get around, but only a cane, then by those observable measures I suppose they are correct.

The initial diagnosis we received that I potentially had a life-threatening illness was mind-numbing to Bonnie and me. The second diagnoses and prognoses for my recovery provided to us by my second neurologist at the University of Utah, Clinical Neurosciences Center, nearly four years ago has been remarkably accurate for the most part.

My recovery, albeit a slow one, has been no less a miracle to me than if I had somehow been born again, both physically and spiritually. I stand in awe at the love of a Heavenly Father who would, from His high place, consider one such as me, in my lowly station, for such a remarkable blessing.

The journey has been the greatest challenge of my life. And this is also true for my amazing companion. We have grown in ways that would likely have not been possible by any other means. Perhaps there are times when God simply has to get our attention. The price of true discipleship is, indeed, priceless.

By all indications it appears that I have recovered as much as I am going to. My body has sustained a certain amount of permanent nerve damage, especially in my legs. I continue to suffer constant pain although it is not nearly as intense or debilitating as it once was. I have regained enough strength in my legs that I am able to walk safely with a single cane which helps to provide me with balance and support for my left leg which hasn't recovered as well as my right leg. However, it's still difficult for me to stand or walk for any significant length of time as the pain increases and my legs weaken. Throughout it all, I have been under the excellent care of two noble physicians who have provided me with outstanding health care in their respective medical specialties.

Much to my chagrin, I am physically unable to return to work. And the prescribed medication I've been given to treat pain from damaged nerves tends to slow my thinking a bit and contribute to drowsiness.

Although I have not been made whole, I am, nonetheless, sincerely grateful for where I am today as compared with where I was just a few short (actually long) years ago.

I continue to write to missionaries but not as many as I once was. As my health slowly improved, I became increasingly able to begin performing household chores. It pleased me greatly to finally be able to take some of the burden off of my beleaguered spouse. At the same time, the number of missionaries serving from our ward increased. This combination of these events was both good and not so good; good in that it meant that I was recovering and more capable of taking on other necessary responsibilities; not so good in that I wasn't able to continue adding new missionaries to my writing list. However, I have committed to continue writing to my existing group of missionaries through the completion of their missions.

What joyful reunions I have had with these young people as they have received honorable releases from their respective fields of labor and returned home to report to the congregation in sacrament meeting. We embrace as great friends in gospel love.

They have experienced great personal growth and maturity. They have gained tremendous gospel and scriptural knowledge, command of language, people skills, and strength of faith, character and testimony. They have been forever changed for the better. Their lives are now centered in the Gospel of Jesus Christ.

And then they move on with their lives, as it should be. They leave their home ward to attend Young Single Adult Wards; they go away for schooling and work. Two of "my missionaries" (so far) have found and married their eternal companions.

No matter where their respective lives take them, I will never forget them nor the impact of the letters of inspiration and healing we shared as our paths crossed for a season.

As always, I remain….

Your brother in the gospel,

Brother Dewey

Appendix A

Dear Elder Wilson:

Congratulations on your recent call to the Seventy. Please know that I fully sustain and support you in your new assignment.

I read with great interest the biographical sketch about you and your lovely wife published in the *Church News* on July 2, 2011. It was wonderful to get better acquainted with you as you begin your service as a General Authority in the Church.

Of particular interest to me was your amazing experience with the mysterious auto-immune disease that caused such havoc to your body and its associated impact on your mind and emotions. I could scarcely believe that someone else had gone through what I am presently experiencing. Although I'm so sorry that you had to live through that terrible and frightening disease, for me to know that someone else has gone through it and recovered to full functionality was exactly what I needed to hear. Although I am not as debilitated as you were, I have a severe peripheral neuropathy which has primarily presented itself in my extremities, especially my feet, legs, and hips. I've lost 60 pounds in just a few months. I am at the worst part of it now and have been told that medical science can do little for me. However, like you, I too now have to wait for my body to heal itself over the next 18 months or so. Your story has given me a tremendous amount of inspiration just at the moment when I needed it most. I can't tell you how much your story has helped me overcome a difficult emotional state. Thanks for sharing it with us.

In the same way that your wife was such a critically important support to you during your ordeal, my wife, Bonnie, has been absolutely wonderful to me during mine. Neither of these good women asked for the difficult duty of caring for us as their lives were turned upside down along with ours, yet they serve us without complaint. We're so fortunate to have them for eternity

Because of my condition, I was released as Stake Sunday School president. I'm 57 years old and I can't remember a time when I didn't have a calling in the Church. Having previously served as high priest group leader in my ward, I particularly miss associating with my group. I have come to know and love these brethren so much.

We have great hope in Christ. I regularly listen to the hymn "How Firm a Foundation" as recorded in the Tabernacle Choir CD *Called to Serve*.[63] One line says, "I'll strengthen thee, help thee, and cause thee to stand, Upheld by my righteous omnipotent hand." I'm counting on this blessing.

Thanks again for inspiring me and God bless you and your wife in your service.

Your brother in Christ,

David Dewey

Appendix B

Unspotted From the World
By Julie Thompson

    A few years ago, I arrived at the Bountiful Utah Temple to fulfill a late-night cleaning assignment. The turnout for the assignment was impressive, and I wondered for a moment if some would be sent home. I was more than ready to volunteer to leave early. Then I cynically thought to myself, *"Of course they won't let us go early. They will find menial jobs for all of us, thinking it was their duty to keep us here for the entire two hours."* I remembered a previous assignment during which I had dusted for more than an hour, only to return a cloth that looked as clean as it had been when it was given to me. I prepared myself to spend two hours cleaning things that didn't appear to need cleaning. Obviously, I had come to the temple that night out of a sense of duty more than from a desire to serve.

    Our group was led to a small chapel for a devotional. The custodian who conducted the devotional said something that will forever change the way I look at temple cleaning assignments. After welcoming us, he proceeded to explain that we were not there to clean things that didn't need cleaning but to keep the Lord's house from ever becoming dirty. As stewards of one of the most sacred places on earth, we had a responsibility to keep it spotless.

    His message penetrated my heart, and I proceeded to my assigned area with a new enthusiasm to protect the Lord's house. I spent time with a soft-bristled paintbrush, dusting the tiny grooves in door frames, baseboards, and the legs of tables and chairs. Had I been given this assignment on an earlier visit, I might have thought it ridiculous and carelessly brushed over the areas in an effort to appear busy. But this time, I made sure the bristles reached into the tiniest of crevices.

    Because this job was neither physically nor mentally taxing, I was blessed with time to ponder while I worked. I first realized that I never paid attention to such minute details in my own home but cleaned those areas that others would see first, neglecting those known only to members of my family and me.

I next realized that there were times when I had lived the gospel in a similar fashion – living those principles and fulfilling those assignment that were most obvious to those around me while ignoring things that seemed known only to my immediate family – all in full view of members of our ward – but neglected to attend the temple regularly, have personal and family scripture study and prayer, and hold family home evening. I taught lessons and spoke in church but sometimes lacked true charity in my heart when it came to interactions with others.

That night in the temple, I studied the paintbrush in my hand and asked myself, *"What are the little crevices in my life that need more attention?"* I resolved that rather than plan to repeatedly clean the areas of my life that needed attention, I would try harder never to let them become dirty.

I remember my temple-cleaning lesson each time we are reminded to keep ourselves *"unspotted from the world"* (James 1:27).

Ensign Magazine, July 2012

Notes

[1] Wendy Ulrich, *The Temple Experience, Passages to Healing and Holiness* (Springville: CFI, 2012).192-193.

[2] In *C.S. Lewis: LDS Perspectives on the Man and His Message* (Brigham Young University, Provo: Covenant Communications, 2006), DVD.

[3] In Conference Report, Oct. 1936, 22.

[4] *Hymns of the Church of Jesus Christ of Latter-day Saints* (Salt Lake City: The Church of Jesus Christ of Latter-day Saints, 1985), no. 85. Emphasis added.

[5] Church News, *Deseret News*, 2 Jul. 20121: C2. Print.

[6] Robert L. Millet, *Coming to Know Christ* (Salt Lake City: Desert Book Company, 2012), 60, 66.

[7] Wendy Ulrich, *The Temple Experience, Passages to Healing and Holiness* (Springville: CFI, 2012), 150-151.

[8] In *C.S. Lewis: LDS Perspectives on the Man and His Message* (Brigham Young University, Provo: Covenant Communications, 2006), DVD.

[9] C. S. Lewis, *Mere Christianity* (San Francisco: HarperCollins, 1952, 1980), 201-2.

[10] Ibid., 205-6.

[11] In *C.S. Lewis: LDS Perspectives on the Man and His Message* (Brigham Young University, Provo: Covenant Communications, 2006), DVD.

[12] Private communication, used with permission.

[13] Ibid.

[14] Michelle King, "Danny Berger's Comeback, 'Mormon Times TV'," *Deseret News*, 11 Apr. 2013: C2. Print.

15 Se4e 1 Nephi 11:16-17.

16 In Conference Report, Oct. 2011.

17 See 2 Nephi 2:25.

18 See Matthew 25:21.

19 See Matthew 7:14; 3 Nephi 14:14; Doctrine and Covenants 132:22; 3 Nephi 27:33.

20 Dallin H. Oaks, *Life's Lessons Learned* (Salt Lake City: Deseret Book, 2011), 102.

21 Ibid., 97-99.

22 Bob Lonesberry, *Hopiland Christmas* (Springville: CFI, 2007). Emphasis added.

23 Ibid.

24 C. Max Caldwell, *Power from on High, Gaining Spiritual Strength* (American Fork: Covenant Communications, 2008).

25 See Moroni 10.

26 See *Preach My Gospel, A Guide to Missionary Service* (Salt Lake City: The Church of Jesus Christ of Latter-day Saints, 2004), 31.

27 John A. Widstow, editor, *Discourses of Brigham Young* (Salt Lake City: Deseret Book Company, June 1954), 456.

28 See Abraham 3:22, Doctrine and Covenants 138:55.

29 See Moroni 10:4.

30 Lynn A. McKinlay, *Life Eternal* (Young People's Temple Group, 1950), 154-155.

31 Julie Thompson, "Unspotted From The World," *Ensign*, Jul., 2012. Used by permission from IRI and the author.

32 C. Terry Warner, *Bonds That Make Us Free* (Salt Lake City: Shadow Mountain, 2001), 44, 113.

33 Ibid., 219, 22, 41, 104, 108. Emphasis added.

34 Ibid., 194.

35 Ibid., 75.

36 In *C.S. Lewis: LDS Perspectives on the Man and His Message* (Brigham Young University, Provo: Covenant Communications, 2006), DVD.

37 See Mosiah 3:19; D&C 67:12; I Corinthians 2:14; Alma 26:21.

38 C. Terry Warner, *Bonds That Make Us Free* (Salt Lake City: Shadow Mountain, 2001), 44.

39 See Alma 5.

40 Dallin H. Oaks, "The Challenge to Become," *Ensign*, Nov., 2002.

41 Robert L. Millet, *Coming to Know Christ* (Salt Lake City: Desert Book Company, 2012), 46, 144-45. Emphasis added.

42 Wendy Ulrich, *The Temple Experience, Passages to Healing and Holiness* (Springville: CFI, 2012), 192.

43 *Preach My Gospel* (Salt Lake City: The Church of Jesus Christ of Latter-day Saints, 2004), 73.

44 David J. Ridges, *65 Signs of the Times Leading Up to the Second Coming* (Springville: CFI, 2009), 180.

45 Dallin H. Oaks, "Powerful Ideas," *Ensign,* Nov. 1995, 25.

46 *Teachings of the Prophet Joseph Smith,* selected and arranged by Joseph Fielding Smith (Salt Lake City: Deseret Book, 1976), 348.

47 Alma 34:33, 36. Emphasis added.

48 David J. Ridges, *65 Signs of the Times Leading Up to the Second Coming* (Springville: CFI, 2009), 183.

49 Marvin J. Ashton, "On Being Worthy," *Ensign*, Apr., 1989, as quoted in Ridges, *65 Signs*. Emphasis added.

50 Craig James Ostler, *Refuge from the Storm* (American Fork, Covenant Communication, 2012), 82.

51 B. H Roberts, *A Comprehensive History of the Church* (Provo: BYU Press, 1957, 1965, 1976), Vol. 4, 540.

52 Melvin J. Ballard, *The Three Degrees of Glory, A Discourse* (Salt Lake City: Deseret Book, 1922), 23.

53 *Gospel Principles* (Salt Lake City: The Church of Jesus Christ of Latter-day Saints), 2011, 243.

54 *Gospel Doctrine*, 5th ed. (Salt Lake City: The Church of Jesus Christ of Latter-day Saints), 1939, 461.

55 *Teachings of Presidents of the Church: Joseph F. Smith*, (2011), 407–15

56 Neal A. Maxwell, *Notwithstanding My Weaknesses* (Salt Lake City: Deseret Book, 1981).

57 Melvin J. Ballard, *The Three Degrees of Glory, A Discourse* (Salt Lake City: Deseret Book, 1922), 23-24.

58 Andrew C. Skinner, *Temple Worship, 20 Truths That Will Bless Your Lives* (Salt Lake City: Deseret Book, 2007), 145.

59 See Abraham 3:22, D&C 138:55.

60 See Mosiah 8:15-17.

61 William R. Bradford, "Sanctification Through Missionary Service", General Conference, Oct., 1981.

62 Donald A. Parry, *Angels - Agents of Light, Love, and Power* (Salt Lake City, Deseret Book, 2013).

[63] Mormon Tabernacle Choir, *Called to Serve* (Salt Lake City: Intellectual Reserve), 2008.

About the Author

David S. Dewey was born and raised in northern Utah. He obtained a business degree from the University of Utah and worked in the banking profession for more than three decades.

He was a member of the Board of Trustees of Salt Lake County Service Area #2 and of the Olympic Speed Skating Oval Management Committee prior to the 2002 Winter Olympic Games held in Salt Lake City.

As a young man, he served an honorable full-time mission for the Church of Jesus Christ of Latter-day Saints in northern England under the leadership, tutelage and watchful care of President Royden G. Derrick and Sister Allie O. Derrick with whom he has remained lifelong friends. He has served on two stake high councils, in a bishopric, as stake mission president, and several times each as high priest group leader and gospel doctrine instructor.

He is married to the former Bonnie Davies. They have three children, four grandchildren, and make their home in West Jordan, Utah.

"I exhort you to sweep the earth with messages filled with righteousness and truth – messages that are authentic, edifying and praiseworthy – and literally to sweep the earth as with a flood." (Elder David A. Bednar of the Quorum of the Twelve Apostles, *Prophet and Apostles Speak*, LDS.org)

The author/copyright holder may be contacted at Lettersih@gmail.com. Discount pricing may be available for orders of five or more soft-cover copies.

www.ingramcontent.com/pod-product-compliance
Lightning Source LLC
Chambersburg PA
CBHW060948050426
42337CB00052B/1875